Introducing

The

Yellowstone

Trail

A Good Road From Plymouth Rock to Puget Sound 1912-1930

I0132639

This is the story of a group of small town businessmen in South Dakota who undertook an ambitious project to create a useful automobile route, the Yellowstone Trail, across America. This was at a time when roads weren't marked, there were few maps and slippery mud was the usual road surface. The Yellowstone Trail Association located a route, motivated road improvements, produced maps and folders to guide the traveler, and promoted tourism along its length. It became a leader in stimulating tourist travel to the Northwest and motivating good roads across America. Today, almost all of the route is on slower, less traveled roads. Some sections of the Trail in the West have remained little changed and are a delight to visit.

Alice A. Ridge   John Wm. Ridge

Second Edition ©2014 by Alice A. Ridge and John Wm. Ridge. All rights reserved. No part of this book may be used or reproduced in any manner whatso-
ever without written permission except in the case of brief quotations embodied
in critical articles and reviews. For information contact the authors through:
www.yellowstonetrail.org
Printed (on demand) by CreateSpace, an Amazon company
First Edition ©2000
Printed by Hignell Printing Limited, Winnipeg

The underlying map data for the state maps were provided by Geographic Data
Technology, Inc (GDT) of Lebanon, NH. The changes to those data, including,
but not limited to, the removing of selected city names, the addition of names of
towns along the Trail and the addition of the route of the Trail are
copyright © 2000 by Alice A. Ridge and John Wm. Ridge.

Editing assistance was provided by Holliday A. Jones

Publishers Cataloging in Publication

Alice A. Ridge and John Wm. Ridge
Introducing the Yellowstone Trail; A Good Road from Plymouth Rock to Puget
    Sound, 1912-1930.
        96 p. : ill. ; 22 x 14 cm.
ISBN 978-0-9702832-4-5

1. Roads--United States--History--20th Century
2. Yellowstone Trail Association (U.S.)
3. Yellowstone Trail--History
4. Automobile Travel--U.S.--Guidebooks

HE356. Y4 R48   2014
388.11 R

Yellowstone Trail Publishers
PO Box 65, Altoona WI 54720-0065
www.yellowstonetrail.org
715 834 5992

Introducing

The Yellowstone Trail

A Good Road From Plymouth Rock to Puget Sound
1912-1930

Contents

Chapter 1. 1912 Creating the Yellowstone Trail............. 1
Chapter 2. 1913 - 1915 The Trail Grows Up 13
Chapter 3. 1916 - 1920 The Formative Years 33
Chapter 4. 1921 - 1925 The Grand Years........................ 47
Chapter 5. 1926 - 1930 The End of the Trail 63
Chapter 6. Driving the Trail Today 75

Maps

USA...................................... iv
Home of the Trail 8
Cross Country Trails 30
Washington.........................76
Idaho/Montana 80
Dakotas 84
Minnesota...........................85
Wisconsin...........................87
Illinois/Indiana 88
Ohio/Pennsylvannia 89
New York 90
Massachusetts 91

The Route of the Yellowstone Trail

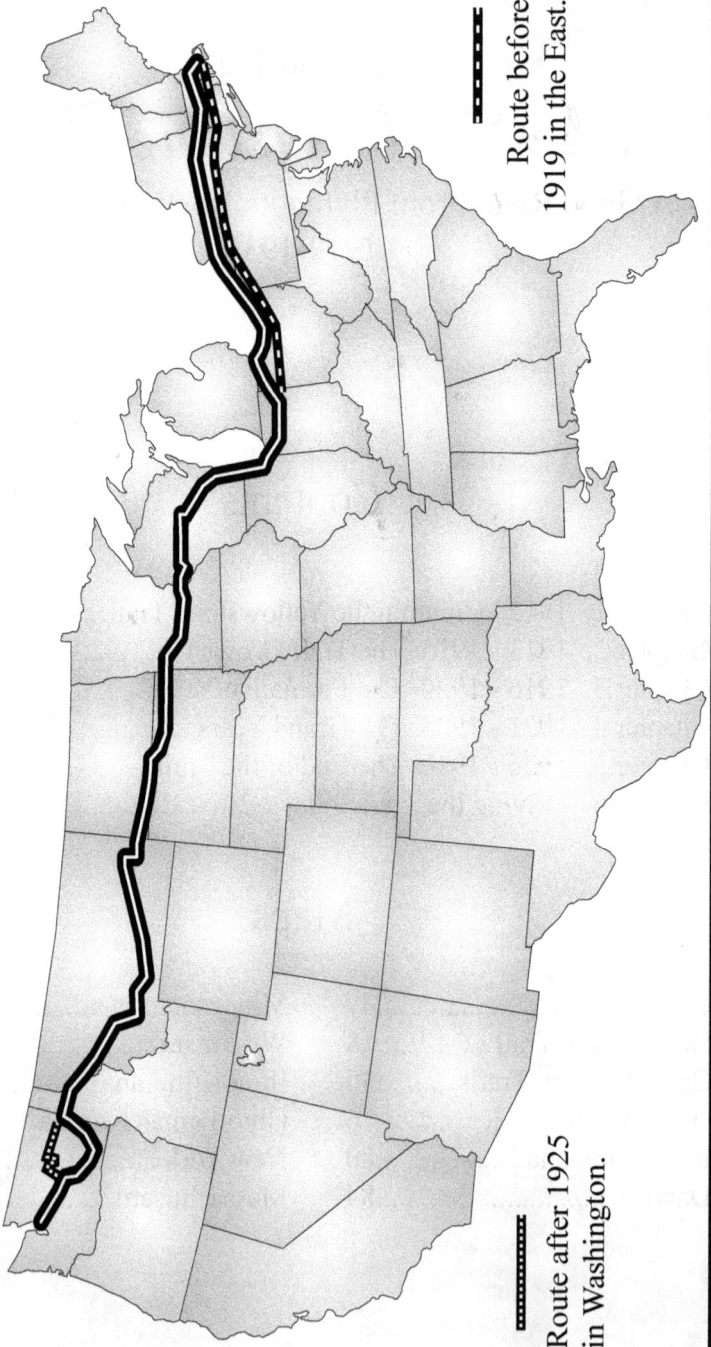

Route before 1919 in the East.

Route after 1925 in Washington.

Chapter One

1912 - Creating the Yellowstone Trail

Joe Parmley was stuck again in the quagmire of the road through Helgerson Slough. There was no way he could rock his car out of it this time. He had neglected to put his chains and planks in the auto. The mud was too deep anyway. Parmley must have considered his grim options: get out and dig (not much hope there), slog through the mud to the nearby farm house and pay the gleeful farmer to pull him out (highway robbery), or sit and wait until someone with auto or horse came by (that could take hours). Those were the only choices available in 1912.

He probably had many thoughts about the road, none of them good. The stream that fed that slough should be dammed. This road between Ipswich and Aberdeen, South Dakota should be better than it was. Twenty-six miles of mud every time it rained, 26 miles of ruts and dust in the dry times. And in the winter? Just forget it and hitch up the sleigh.

It is hard for the modern reader to even imagine a world without good roads or good signs to guide the way, or road maps. Can you imagine yourself on a prairie grass or dirt road with a farmer's fence across your path? Mountainous terrains with narrow ruts cut into near-vertical sides would present quite a challenge to a generation weaned on the Interstate system. Modern readers need imagination to comprehend the immobility of it all.

Autos, Railroads and Roads

Before the advent of automobiles, many roads were created simply through repeated use by horses and wagons. Unpaved roads were suited to ironclad hooves and wagon wheels. The wheels of a horse-drawn vehicle turn because the wagon is being pulled. Wheels have little disturbing effect on the roadbed except in wet weather and on sharp turns. In winter, farmers replaced wheels with sled runners, riding on top of the snow, producing even less effect on the road. Auto tires, however, with their greater speed and the fact that they were providing the driving force, sucked gravel and dirt off the roads, thus destroying the surface and stirring up great clouds of dust.

But people bought automobiles at a dizzying pace, in spite of the miserable road conditions and the snail's pace of road construction. In 1912 there were 356,000 autos sold in the U.S. Sales reached almost a million in 1915.[1] All those car tires chewed up what roads there were.

Joe Parmley had been seriously concerned about bad roads for years. As a founder of the little town of Roscoe, South Dakota, in 1883, Joe had watched farm wagons too slowly work their way over the prairies to the grain elevator. It was costing farmers more to get their products to the train over poor roads than it was to ship them to Chicago. In 1907 Joe had been hooted down in the South Dakota legislature for his novel suggestion that people should pay their township road taxes in cash and not by working on the road. This road work, or *corvee* system, was a joke and everybody knew it. Yet, legislators were loathe to institute cash taxes. A popular poem at the time depicted the general opinion that the *corvee* was often just a holiday for shovel-leaners:

> Our life is tough and fearful
> > Its toil was often tearful
> And often we grew faint beneath the load.
> > But there came a glad vacation
> And a sweet alleviation
> > When we used to work our tax out on the road [2]

Six years later his idea was adopted and praised, but Joe Parmley had long since moved on in his thinking about roads. He now envisioned a network of roads that actually went somewhere, a network that might cross more than one state, a network that may even span a nation.

Pre-automobile trails had been known since before Northern Europeans arrived in the U.S. The Santa Fe Trail in the New Mexico, Texas, Oklahoma area was traveled by Mexican priests, traders and trappers. The Old Spanish Trail from Florida to Louisiana was traversed by Spaniards and Indians. Indian trails everywhere preceded any European effort. The dangerous Bozeman Trail through Wyoming and Montana in the 1800's was used by westward-bound settlers and traders who risked Indian attacks regularly.

The federal government had perceived very early the need for roads as part of the country's transportation infrastructure. The National Road, also called the Cumberland Road and the National Pike, was begun in 1811 by the government. It ran from Maryland to Vandalia, Illinois where the support and the road alike stopped. Many military roads, such as the Mullan road in the Northwest, were mapped and built in the mid-1800's. However, government involvement in roads essentially ceased with the coming of the railroad and canals. The country grew to rely almost exclusively on the rails for both freight and passenger service. The railroad built the West. Roads were needed only within towns and between the farmer's field and the nearest railway stop.

In the late 1800's, owners of the newfangled bicycles, and in the opening years of the 1900's, owners of automobiles became strong proponents of good roads. But the country had no established government responsibility or funding for roads.

In 1912, there was little hope for state or federal money for any road. By that year the human landscape of much of the country from the Midwest through the plains to the Pacific was being, and had been, created by the railroad industry. Railroads extended track west, created towns along the route, named the new towns after their company president's daughter or uncle, found immigrants and others to live in those towns, then benefited by the shipments of goods to the towns and from farm products sent back to the cities. The railroads quickly annihilated the wagon trains, the pony express, canals and the need for long-distance roads.

Federal government policy supported the railroads through huge land grants. Previous limited federal attempts to construct long-distance roads and military roads quickly disappeared. The "road" meant the railroad in newspaper headlines; a map meant a railroad map; travel even to nearby towns meant travel by train. Some towns might have three or four or more trains stopping every day. Small town America swayed to the rhythm of the train schedule. Stores, hotels and brothels were located near the tracks, and hours of business were set by the train schedule. The depot was the center of life, where brass bands played, where little family dramas played out every day, where the telegrapher was the newscaster, and where packages arrived from Sears and Roebuck.

The country was totally unprepared for the sudden appearance of the automobile and its overwhelming popularity. Automobile roads were in abysmal shape or nonexistent, especially west of the Mississippi. One of the first organized efforts to improve roads came in 1892 when Charles L. Burdet, head of the League of American Wheelmen, an organization of four million bicyclists, argued that "There is no class in the community to whom the necessity of better roads is more apparent than the presidents of the great interior transportation lines." [3] The better the feeder roads from farm

A typical Good Roads train.   *Photo courtesy of the Federal Highway Administration*

to railhead, the more freight that could be moved. It would also be cheaper for the farmer and all would benefit. If the roads were so bad that farmers could not afford to move products to the railhead, or to move products from the railhead back to the farm, all would suffer. So effective were the bicyclists' appeals and the railhead economic argument, that western railroads readily lent their support to new road projects. Among other things, they transported, free of charge, demonstration road equipment. This appeared to have been a good public relations move, considering all of the bad press railroads had been receiving concerning their monopolistic attitudes toward freight and postal rates and the public in general.

Courtesy of the Mineral County [MT] Museum

In 1901, the railroads joined with the National Good Roads Association and its persuasive promoter, Colonel William Moore, in producing a traveling good roads show. Trains were loaded with road building equipment and experts who built sample one-mile demonstration roads in the Midwest. Lectures on road building accompanied the demonstrations. Good Roads trains were followed, in the 1910's and 1920's, by Good Roads Schools which were held on university campuses and which were attended by rural engineers, county commissioners, city engineers, and others. Demonstrations and lectures

Courtesy of the J.W. Parmley Historical Museum, Ipswich

in drainage, bituminous construction and concrete roads filled two days. Announcements of coming Good Roads Schools hit all of the papers along the Yellowstone Trail.

In spite of the efforts of Good Roads Trains, Good Roads Associations, The Wheelmen, and dozens of congressional bills, federal aid for roads was terribly slow in coming. Our nation had no infrastructure to establish roads because roads were interpreted as being "internal improvements" and, therefore, possibly unconstitutional. Finally, in 1912, money for post roads was appropriated, but a haphazard, unconnected pattern of roads often resulted. The 1916 and 1921 federal-aid acts apportioned more money for post roads. By this time Rural Free Delivery (RFD) was two decades old and almost all roads were designated as post roads.

A Grass Roots Movement

During 1912, Parmley felt that the only way to get the 26-mile long road, or any road, improved was through a grass roots movement. An organization was needed to select the most promising existing roads or paths in a town or township, connect them to the most

"Roads, Beginning Nowhere, Ending Nowhere." This poster shows 4,608 miles of unconnected star and rural free delivery post roads in Wyoming that the National Highways Association believed needed to be connected through a policy of federally built and maintained highways.

promising roads in the next township or county and eventually establish a single route with a single name that went a long distance. The representatives of this organization would have to persuade county governments along the route to spend road dollars on a proper single route instead of just patching random roads. A single good road would soon create feeder roads, Parmley hypothesized, and a network of county roads would result, leading to a state trunk road system - or perhaps even more.

It was against this backdrop of frustration at the lack of decent roads and the lack of state and federal help that convinced Joe Parmley, Marcus Beebe and others that they had no one to rely on but themselves. The organization of road enthusiasts that they envisioned was begun in Ipswich, South Dakota on a rainy April 23, 1912. The Commercial Club rooms were packed with 100 men from five counties to hear noted Good Roads Association and Grange speakers. But, most of all, they came to *do* something. These men were very aware of the value of roads and the value of publicity to a town situated on a well-traveled road. They all had heard of the slogan: Get us out of the mud.

Their first target for improvement was that 26 miles of poor road between Ipswich and Aberdeen. To travel that road was to risk that marsh which some called the "Slough of Despond." There was a crude bridge, but one end led to a steep hill and the other a sharp curve. Gumbo, a slimy, gluey, viscous mud, lay in places very thick, and in summer if it didn't rain, dust lay in some places inches deep.

By all accounts the Ipswich meeting was electric and productive; by the end of that day the group had:

• Formed the Northern Development League of the South Dakota Development Association, electing Parmley as President

• Established a road building committee of 15 to work with three county boards to raise money for the 26-mile improvement and to establish a route between Aberdeen and Mobridge on the Missouri River

• Voted to name that 26-mile route "Parmley Highway." Parmley demurred.

• Decided to sponsor an automobile "run" from Aberdeen to Mobridge to find a route, inspect the existing road, and publicize the effort.

So enthusiastic became Ipswich banker Marcus Beebe that he marched into the Edmunds County Board meeting, plunked down $500 seed money for improvements on that 26-mile "Parmley Road" and promised another $500 to help build and improve connecting roads.

South Dakota had no provision for state aid to counties for roads yet.

New Jersey created the idea in 1891 for a state to fund county roads on a 67% county-33% state basis. The idea was popular, although all states did not follow New Jersey's lead, including South Dakota, claiming poverty or state constitutional limits on "internal improvements." The same thinking also kept South Dakota from participating in the 1912 Federal Post Office Appropriations Act which gave states aid toward the cost of building post roads on a 1/3 federal government-2/3 state basis. Aid for any roads or bridges still had to be doubled from local road taxes, which South Dakota was unwilling to do.

While three South Dakota county boards scrambled to respond to the new pressure to invest all available money in improving only one road, plans went ahead for a June two-day "sociability run" to Mobridge, 100 miles west of Aberdeen. A sociability run was a popular social event that involved food, gaiety, and a string of cars being driven somewhere together. Ostensibly, 'runs' were formed to examine a road, or to test the endurance of different makes of cars, or to inaugurate anything communities wanted inaugurated. A good time was had by all. The run to Mobridge featured state engineer S.H. Lea who laid out a route and examined approaches to the precipitous drop into the Missouri River Valley.

The hyperbolic description of the days' events occupied the entire front page of the July 25, 1912 *Ipswich Tribune* and ended with a prophetic comment. The reporter opined that this 100-mile road would be "a section of a great national highway connecting the cities of the east coast with those of the west coast and Plymouth Rock on the east and Puget Sound on the west."[4] Either that reporter was a poet with an ear for balance and alliteration and created the phrase, or he picked it up from Parmley or auto enthusiasts. Wherever it originated, the phrase "A Good Road from Plymouth Rock to Puget Sound," through the power of the press, was now being talked about by commercial clubs and development leagues in the area. The phrase eventually became the motto of the Yellowstone Trail Association, appearing on all of the maps, brochures, letterheads and official statements of the group.

Mobridge Sociability Run   June 20-21, 1912.
First Year Book of the Twin Cities-Aberdeen-Yellowstone Park Trail 1914

By late autumn of 1912 that original 26 miles of road had been "completed," dirt still, but ditched, graded and dragged. Another sociability run with much fanfare, band playing, bunting and food was conducted between Aberdeen and Ipswich to "open" the road.

The Birth of the Yellowstone Trail Association - Oct. 9, 1912

Americans were, and are, noted for their tradition of organizing for every conceivable purpose. As de Tocqueville once said of Americans, " . . . if they are to proclaim a truth, or propagate some feeling by the encouragement of a great example, they form an association."[5] To that end, an organizational meeting was held in Lemmon, South Dakota on October 9 and 10. Lemmon is a small town in the extreme northwest of South Dakota. In 1912 it lay along the Milwaukee Road tracks and served as a shipping point for farmers. F.A. Finch knew a progressive thing when he saw it and invited this new Good Roads group for a meeting. It turned out to be a meeting to form not another of the many Good Roads Association chapters, but to form an organization to push for a single highway from the Twin Cities to Yellowstone Park. Given those parameters, the choice of name for the new group seemed appropriate, although rather long: The Twin Cities-Aberdeen-Yellowstone Park Trail Association. It would be shortened officially to the "Yellowstone Trail Association" in 1915.

Everything about the early Twin Cities-Aberdeen-Yellowstone Park Trail Association spelled grass roots. Thoroughly disgusted with big government inaction, the group believed that a coalition of small towns influencing county boards would succeed in getting one long road. All members were expected to push hard on their local governments, newspapers, and neighbors to support this road. Motivation for towns to join in the effort was two-fold: (1) the use of a good road, and (2) publicity, fortune and tourists. Eventually, towns formed state chapters and voted upon issues of route, publicity, new member towns, and tourist attraction. But most of all, members served to inform Trail officers about route and road improvement

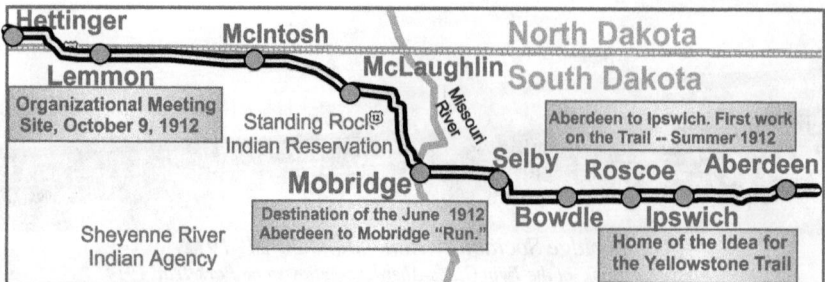

Hettinger

McIntosh   North Dakota

Lemmon   McLaughlin South Dakota

Organizational Meeting
Site, October 9, 1912   Standing Rock
                               Indian Reservation   Aberdeen to Ipswich. First work
                                                           on the Trail -- Summer 1912

                                                 Selby Roscoe   Aberdeen
                      Mobridge

Sheyenne River   Destination of the June 1912   Bowdle   Ipswich
Indian Agency   Aberdeen to Mobridge "Run."
                                                           Home of the Idea for
                                                           the Yellowstone Trail

Yellowstone Trail West of Ipswich, South Dakota. Autumn 1912
Courtesy of J.W. Parmley Historical Museum

options. Members were the eyes and ears of progress.

From the initial dues schedule of $25 per county, $1 per individual member and any donations proffered, the group quickly shifted to a formula of payment of $50 per county, $1 per individual, and each town or automobile organization according to the number of inhabitants or members. This was again changed in a few years, assessing each community depending upon the amount of "benefit that community would accrue from a good road" and from the tourist. Thus, larger cities such as Billings, Montana would be charged $4000 and smaller towns paid about $250. The income was used solely for the administration of the Association and for literature for distribution. No elected officer was paid a salary, but travel expenses to meetings were reimbursed. The Association had no paid lobbyists in the state capitals. In later years, other administrative expenses included such things as maintenance of a headquarters in Minneapolis and a general manager's salary. There were special collections for emergencies such as the need for a bridge over the Little Missouri River at Marmarth, North Dakota and a basic road in Corson County, South Dakota on the Standing Rock Indian Reservation, for which there was no one to pay. These two projects needed completion to close gaps in the Trail, so financial aid to counties was deemed necessary in these cases.

The Yellowstone Trail Association didn't make anyone rich. In fact, at the end of 12 years the General Manager claimed that he had personally paid for a typewriter, and Joe Parmley could claim that he had spent many dollars for chrome yellow paint used to mark rocks and telegraph poles along the way. A good year, 1921, revealed a $40,000 balance which was quickly spent on brochures and maps to give away. Frequently, the organization published glowing figures of the amount spent on a certain portion of the Trail. Since the Yellowstone Trail Association did not *build* roads, those claims may well have been exaggerated. Counties and townships themselves spent the large sums to build the roads. But the Association's local units had often been the persuasive factor. The Association was probably right in its assumption that without the local Trailmen, route committees and boosters that the Association garnered, those roads might never have been built by the counties.

The beginning years of the Trail Association also meant acquiring useable information from each state. In order to establish uniformity in individual state meetings, and in order to get input about outstanding issues, a meeting agenda was issued each year asking for state chapters to respond to such germane questions as: Does your state desire a continuation of active Yellowstone Trail involvement? What should be the marking program for the next year? What should be the Trail improvement program for the next year? Is the Trail properly located in your state? What national or state legislation should we favor or oppose? What should we do about delinquent assessments? What should the costs of the organization be and what share should your state pay? Presuming that the Executive Commit-

Joe Parmley and His Road Drag
First Year Book of the Twin Cities-Aberdeen-Yellowstone Park Trail 1914

Elevating Grader with Steam Tractor   *Eastern Washington University Achives*

tee acted upon advice, one could only conclude that this organization was democratic if nothing else.

The Twin Cities-Aberdeen-Yellowstone Park Trail Association was off and running. By the end of 1912, 100 miles of a single road that actually went somewhere was "paved" with dirt which had been graded and dragged, three counties had worked in harmony to join roads at county lines, and the march to Yellowstone Park was on.

Left, J.W. Parmley, Founder of the Yellowstone Trail Association

Right, H.O.Cooley, General Manager of the Yellowstone Trail Association

Courtesy of
Dr. Joseph Trotzig, Grandson

Courtesy of
Jane Vinger, Granddaughter

Where's the bridge?
Eastern Washington University Archives

Endnotes

1. Motor Vehicle Manufacturing Association of the U.S., <u>Automobiles of America</u> (Detroit: Wayne State University Press, 1974) 283.

2. J. H. McKeever, "How Good Roads Came to South Dakota," <u>Better Roads</u> Oct. 1969:19.

3. Albert A. Pope, <u>Wagon Roads as Feeders to Railways</u> (Boston, 1892) 8 cited in Oscar O. Winther, <u>The Transportation Frontier: Trans-Mississippi West 1865-1890.</u> (Chicago: Holt Rinehart and Winston, 1964) 154.

4. <u>Ipswich Tribune</u> July 25, 1912:1.

5. Alexis de Tocqueville as quoted in Bradley J. Birzer, "Expanding Creative Destruction: Entrepreneurship in the American Wests," <u>The Western Historical Quarterly</u> 30:1,(Spring 1999) 513.

Chapter Two

1913-1915 The Trail Grows Up

The Yellowstone Trail Association was firmly established. The founders and the members alike had no doubt about their ability to create a great road. The commitment was there to extend the marked Trail as quickly as there were roads to run it on, to share knowledge of road building and lobbying, and to motivate tourism on the Trail through nation-wide publicity. Those things were accomplished during 1913-1915.

First Annual Convention - February 17, 1913

Miles City, Montana was and still is an interesting, historic town. In 1913 it was a center for cattle trading and shipping and had a reputation as a "wild and woolly" town. Montana Bar, reminiscent of those days, can still be seen on Main Street. Although the Northern Pacific was the first railroad through the city, the Milwaukee Road Railroad promoted the town vigorously and helped prompt a boom economy. With two rail companies serving the town, a road approaching from the north and another from Billings and other points west, it was no more than the usual trouble for the delegates of the Yellowstone Trail Association to get to Miles City for the first annual convention. Presided over by President Marcus Beebe, the Ipswich banker, and Vice President, J.E. Prindle, a land dealer from Ismay, Montana, the Yellowstone Trail organization began to take shape on February 17th, 1913, giving form to function.

First, the delegates to the convention created an organizational structure. In addition to the officers, the structure included provisions for a field agent, route committees, local Trailmen (liaisons between communities and headquarters) and a publicity committee. While the purposes were not specifically enumerated, the records of the meeting make it clear that the Association wished to:

1. Establish and map a route along existing roads from the Twin Cities (Minneapolis and St. Paul, Minnesota) to the Yellowstone National Park. This was their most important goal and was soon to be extended.

2. Advocate good roads by undertaking the construction and repair of roads, teaching road construction, and urging financial support from various levels of government. Promoting government funding soon dominated this second purpose and established the method of acquiring a transcontinental road.

3. Attract and motivate tourist traffic to boost economic development and improve the image of towns along the Trail. This would be done by providing free maps, travel literature and information and news releases. This third purpose established an important reason for communities to embark upon this enterprise.

4. Promote a vision of a nation webbed with roads good in all seasons running transcontinentally north and south and east and west to be planned and built with an amalgam of governmental and citizenry input.

Official statements from the Association reflected an essential regional concept, but newspaper reports of the meetings and other discussions made it clear that the founders had a coast-to-coast concept. Seven months before the first annual meeting in Miles City the phrase "from Plymouth Rock to Puget Sound" had been reported (see Chapter 1). Of the Miles City meeting, a reporter for the *Aberdeen News* declared that the organization would "do all in its power to convert this trail into a great interstate highway with the ultimate end in view of securing a coast- to-coast highway along this route from New York [sic.] to the Pacific."[1]

It must be surmised that the founders of the Trail had a clear vision of a coast to coast highway. It is also reasonable that the founders understood that the funding, the labor, the commitment, the enthusiasm had to come from hundreds or thousands along the route. The founders also seemed to understand that the structure of the Association would do well to remain a grass roots and local or regional movement to keep motivated the vast number of people it needed to succeed. The official actions taken at meetings of the Association through the years reflected this regional concept of the Trail. The Association chose quiet leadership in which they worked to get members to create and assume ownership of the "great ideas," thus motivating commitment; each portion of the Trail affected all the other portions. This approach was apparent in the subsequent operations of the association: great attention was paid to making the Association democratic, but the constraints on the democratic decisions were always well apparent. For example, local locating committees were given nearly absolute authority to decide upon the local route, with the approval of county officials, but decisions about which towns were to be included on the route were made by the national Association's Executive Committee.

The Association spent most of 1913 locating the Trail between the Twin Cities and Yellowstone Park. The work of local locating committees was reported in detail by local newspapers as the Trail expanded both east and west from its beginning in South Dakota. A sample of this interest follows from the *Aberdeen American* of April 18, 1913:

> The South Dakota locating committee for the Twin Cities-Aberdeen-Yellowstone Park Trail left this morning at 9:30 in G.A. Sunstrum's new machine with Mr. Sunstrum driving, for Ortonville, Minnesota to locate the Trail between this city and the Minnesota state line mile by mile. At Ortonville the locators will meet a party which leaves Granite Falls to locate the Minnesota Trail from there to the South Dakota state line. The two delegations will hold a meeting tomorrow evening in Ortonville and officially route the Trail for every mile of the way from Granite Falls west to this city.

Similarly, the *Rhame* (North Dakota) *Review* of June 26 reported that "surveyors for the Yellowstone Trail had been working in the vicinity." The article continued, excitedly reporting each section line that would carry the Trail. And so it went as groups determined which roads the Trail should follow from the Twin Cities to Yellowstone Park. Of course, county boards had yet to be consulted, and county funds needed to be allocated to improve the existing roads.

Second Annual Convention February 20-21, 1914

The second annual meeting of the Yellowstone Trail Association was held in Mobridge, South Dakota, a relatively new town without a highway bridge across the mighty Missouri River, and no decent road to the west. The Milwaukee Road did have a railroad bridge at Mobridge (from which the town name was derived–Missouri River bridge) and the company allowed autos across it at times. It probably was a dangerous, rough ride. Two ferry companies operated across the river at Mobridge. The river in 1914 was narrower and faster before they completed the dam that created the very long Lake Oahe and forced a relocation of the Trail on the west side of the river..

Two new people were asked at this second annual meeting to join the Yellowstone Trail Association staff. Rev. George Keniston, a noted

Chatauqua speaker, was hired for four months as a financial agent who would travel along the Trail and encourage town governments, commercial clubs and businessmen to join the Association and to pay dues. He was also charged to accept donations for the special projects of building the Marmarth, North Dakota bridge over the Little Missouri River and the road in Corson County, South Dakota, a practically uninhabited area with limited support from the federal Bureau of Indian Affairs. An estimated $40,000 was needed to help these two counties.

The other decision of lasting effect was to add Harold O. Cooley to the staff of unpaid workers as Commissioner of Publicity. This was the first of many positions held by Cooley within the Association over the years, receiving a salary finally in 1916. Prior to 1914 he had been secretary of the Aberdeen Auto Club and active in civic affairs. He was very familiar with the operations of the Association. He was also a salesman *par excellence*. Energetic to a fault, totally devoted to his task, a quick study of men, and very funny. For the next 16 years he visited local and state Yellowstone Trail organizations across the nation delivering speeches filled with facts wrapped up in humorous tales. Newspapers of the time usually described his appearances as enlightening and very entertaining. And often very long.

Semi-Annual convention - August 1914

Hunters Hot Springs was a substantial spa center in 1914 with a large resort hotel, sanitarium, and hot springs. It was half way between Big Timber and Livingston, just north of tiny Springdale. Today the traveler does not see much, just weeds that have grown up around the remains of building foundations and some stone walls. The visitor today can sit on bits of rubble, ponder the demise of this popular place, and hear the Montana wind whisper of days gone by.

This setting served as a meeting place of the Association six months after the second annual meeting. The atmosphere must have been mercurial. The main topic was the extension of the Trail westward beyond Yellowstone Park. It seemed that every Montana member had an opinion. A very vocal contingent from Great Falls held the floor often and had to be gaveled down repeatedly. They desired the Trail to come their way and to enter Glacier Park. Many others saw a route through Three Forks, Butte, Missoula, and across the Bitterroots near St. Regis to be the best. The two-day argument was settled when Mr. Goddard declared that the Montana Highway Commission had selected the Three Forks-Butte-Missoula routes to be a state route and would put money into its developing. It was settled. And, indeed, the route did go that way.

Trail Day at Marmarth, North Dakota
First Year Book of the Twin Cities-Aberdeen-Yellowstone Park Trail 1914

Yellowstone Trail Days

The idea of a "citizen road work day" was borrowed from the Good Roads Association which had been active for decades. Lunch was made by the women, stores closed, men brought shovels, teams of horses and road drags, and the county sometimes provided materials. It was a good excuse to get out, have a picnic, and socialize with neighbors. In 1914 Trail Day was May 22.

The object of such an undertaking was, of course, to get the road repaired. But if carried out successfully, it would give the Yellowstone Trail a reputation and standing before the country that money could not buy. The planners figured that a spectacle of an army of 100,000 men all working in concert on a road more than 1100 miles long would be an achievement that would make the Yellowstone Trail a household word. The press was alerted. Word was sent to all state, county and township officials, to the newspapers along the Trail, and to the Trailmen. The announcement by Secretary O.T. Peterson was dramatic, patriotic, and even smacked of Crusaders setting out on a holy mission.

Shortly before the event, J.W. Parmley issued suggestions for proceeding so that a uniform product would result: mark the Trail with a foot-high yellow band around poles; repair dangerous culverts, bridges or grades and place proper warnings at turns or railway crossings; drain or grade sloughs for the traveler to have a solid foundation; drag every mile of the Trail with a split log or other drag; grade and gravel as much of the Trail as possible; remove all stones larger than a walnut and remove rubbish; finish all work undertaken. Parmley also invited anyone "clothed with authority to use their official positions to aid in making this . . . the great highway of the continent."[2]

And did they turn out for the event? Absolutely. The best fed group seemed to have been the 250 men at Hettinger, North Dakota. They consumed 30 gallons of baked beans, 30 gallons of potato salad, 1500 sandwiches, 70 gallons of lemonade, several boxes of apples - and 200 cigars. The six men who marked the Trail omitted nothing: telephone poles, lamp posts, fence posts, and hundreds of stones erected along twelve miles of highway. Although prohibited from the topic of politics, gubernatorial candidates spoke, extra paint was ordered by merchants, cement posts suitable for markers were placed in Gascoyne, North Dakota, and many miles of road were plowed, graded, and made ready for dragging. And a good time was had by all.[3]

The actual count of workers along that 1100 miles is not known, but according to various weekly newspapers, a good many communities turned out. Some Trail Day events were rained out. Terry, Montana jumped the gun and worked on their Trail in April as well as May. Hettinger, too, had two Trail Days because many farmers were too busy with spring planting to attend the May 22 event. This second event in June was to be filmed with the intention to show the film to towns along the Trail. Citizens were asked to work as diligently as before and to provide some action for the camera; "have a foot race or tug of war; have ladies serve lunch promptly and energetically; bring your equipment as before, have a slush scraper working."[4] The film was never made. In spite of the governor of North Dakota declaring that date to be Good Roads Day, it rained.

The 1915 Trail Day was as successful as 1914, if small town newspaper accounts are to be believed. Trail Days continued for several years before interest flagged. Ipswich, South Dakota revived Trail Days in 1939 as a summer festival, complete with a circus, parade, and historical themes.

The Yellowstone Trail has Competition - 1915

The Yellowstone Trail Association met in Montevideo, Minnesota in February 1915 for its third convention and agreed to extend the Trail to Seattle on the west and to Chicago on the east. Preliminary exploration from Chicago east was undertaken by Vice President M. J. Dowling, but no group action was taken until the next year. The route across the Bitterroots into Idaho was equally perplexing, and Joe Parmley himself was called to the Montana/Idaho border to view the few possible routes. No decision would come until an Executive Committee meeting in October. The name of the Trail was shortened to simply "The Yellowstone Trail" and the motto of "a Good Road from Plymouth Rock to Puget Sound" was formally adopted, having been used by the popular press since 1912.

At that same time, a group of active road enthusiasts had gathered in the state of Washington to form an organization to establish an interstate auto road which would follow the route of the Northern Pacific Railroad, but would also follow much of the present Yellowstone Trail in Montana. In an effort to gain support from Washington for extending the Yellowstone Trail through that state, Trail Secretary O.T. Peterson attended a meeting in Spokane in January. Present were representatives of several Washington auto clubs, such as the Automobile Club of Seattle, Washington State Good Roads Association, Inland Automobile Association, and several chambers of commerce and development leagues. All were in accord about the need for interstate roads, and there was a willingness to entertain an extension of the Yellowstone Trail in Washington. However, A.L. Westgard, a pathfinder sponsored by the American Automobile Association, had previously laid out a trail he called the Northwest Trail which followed on, or north of, the eventual route of the Yellowstone Trail. F.W. Guilbert of Spokane, an energetic leader in all road issues, felt that a new name was needed for this amalgam of his new, as yet unnamed trail, the Northwest Trail and the Yellowstone Trail. He chose the name "National Parks Highway," feeling that the amalgamated road would go through Mt. Rainier Park, Glacier Park and Yellowstone Park, and perhaps others. He had in mind retaining the name Yellowstone Trail for the trail east of Terry, Montana to the Twin Cities. Kalispell, Montana and Washington towns would agree to launch a vast advertising campaign for the newly amalgamated trail.[5] Seattle offered "a carload of split log drags" to be used on the Washington route of the new trail.[6]

Peterson telegraphed the leaders of the Yellowstone Trail Association concerning the proposed name change, and "there was an immediate flood of telegrams from all sections of the Trail in defense of the name Yellowstone Trail. One man wired: I will fight to the last ditch for the name of Yellowstone Trail. The Trail officers have, as a result of these expressions, concluded that it is impossible to change the name. There is too much sentiment connected with it. One might as well suggest to change the name of your city, state or the members of your family."[7] Indeed, the name Yellowstone Trail had already been incorporated into everyday life along much of the Trial including stationery of businesses all along the Trail, yellow stickers slapped on luggage in Livingston, Montana, Bagely Flour sacks imprinted with the Trail in yellow in front of mountainous scenery, the Yellowstone Trail brand of candy produced in Aberdeen, South Dakota, and the Yellowstone Trail brand of road drag.

Some felt that the portion of the route from Minnesota to Washington should be called the Yellowstone Trail and Washington's portion of the Trail could be called Sunset Highway, a route most used then from Spokane to Seattle.

F.W. Guilbert expressed his astonishment that, in his view, an "agreement had already been reached and then the officials of the Yellowstone Trail Association would not agree to a name change."[8]   Because Peterson had sent telegrams asking for opinion and guidance, it does not seem likely that he had agreed to a name change unilaterally, especially since this National Parks Highway Association had not yet been formed and the Yellowstone Trail Association was already over two years old. Thus, the National Parks Highway took one road, and the Yellowstone Trail group took another.

While the route of the National Parks Highway was often modified, it followed much the same route as did the Yellowstone Trail, except in the Dakotas, choosing to follow the Northwest Highway through central North Dakota. It also included a spur running to Kalispell and Glacier Park. Its route across the Idaho/Montana line also changed in consonance with the conditions of three alternative roads. The Yellowstone Trail Association could have looked on the bright side: two major highway associations were advertising the same route.

Guilbert's proposal wasn't the only radical change requested. In 1920 a major push was made by Portland, Oregon, to wrest the terminus of the Trail from Seattle. The Trail Association did not have to go to battle at all, as the Seattle Auto Club defended the Trail thus: "The Yellowstone Trail carries twice as many eastern tourists to Seattle as any other highway. It is in the interest of every Seattleite to block the effort to have the route diverted to Portland."[9] In 1924 Glendive, Montana, once again sought the Trail as it had done 11 years previously, seeking to divert it north to join the National Parks Highway through North Dakota. That attempt also failed. Changes were made aplenty in the route, but none instigated by outside forces succeeded.

The 16 Hour Run Across South Dakota - May 15, 1915

Ever mindful of the value of advertising, and aware of the excitement engendered by auto races and similar stunts, Joe Parmley embarked on a race-against-time across South Dakota to show the practicality of the Yellowstone Trail. Three hundred and forty-nine miles in 16 hours! That's an average of 21.8 miles per hour, without stops for meals and repairs. Could it be done? Parmley's point was that anyone with a good car could do it

Over the Yellowstone Trail

Across South Dakota (349 Miles) in One Day

SAT., MAY 15, 1915

PRESIDENT J. W. PARMLEY

of the Yellowstone Trail Association
will make this trip, accompanied by Newspaper Men

The Car Used is a STUDEBAKER SIX

Under the direction of W. C. NISSEN, Distributor, Aberdeen, S. D.

The one car making the entire run.   Car is equipped with Racine Country
Road Tires and carrying appropriate banners.

Part of a Yellowstone Trail Association poster. It continued with a
detailed schedule of the run across the state, including:
Leave Lemmon - 4:00A.M.; Mobridge - 9:30 A.M.;
Aberdeen - 1:50 P.M.; Arrive - Big Stone - 8:00 P.M.

because the Trail was in good condition.

"Anyone" did not have a specially equipped car, a professional driver, relief drivers at the ready, roads cleared for their race, a mechanic, or "mechanician" as they were then called, on board, "pit crews" armed, and the press clocking their every inch and telegraphing their progress to the next town, not to mention crowds at each town complete with brass bands. Parmley made plans for the attack that any general would be proud of.

The route was to be from Lemmon in the far northwest of South Dakota to Big Stone City on the east border of South Dakota. The day selected was a Saturday to maximize crowd attendance. A single car, rather than relay cars, was selected "to make it more interesting." The car chosen was a heavy Studebaker Six supplied by W.C. Nissen, a Studebaker dealer from Aberdeen. "When the trip was planned, the car was stripped of its windshield and top and was covered about its body with a canvas cover on which was painted signs."[10]

The driver was M.B. Payne who had driven in two Glidden tours (cross country runs sponsored by AAA). Telegrams were to be sent to all commercial clubs along the Trail as the car proceeded. All was in readiness - except for the weather. It had rained the day before and sporadically that day. Apparently the party was loathe to postpone such an adventure, and/or they had faith in the Trail shedding water, because Payne and Parmley set off as planned at 4:00 A.M. from Lemmon.

Excited newspaper accounts of the trip used such terms as "skidding through," "streaking by," "tearing along," "flying trip" and "wild ride." The speedometer did hit 60 at one point, a remarkable feat. The breathless accounts may have titillated their readers, but the present day reader gets a picture quite different. The Studebaker plowed through mud almost all of the way, mud from four to ten inches deep in some places. Parmley later described their progress as looking like a torpedo boat, throwing wings of mud like a marine manure spreader. Chains applied to the tires broke repeatedly. Parmley intended to use a dictagraph to dictate observations on the trip; after the first severe bump, all thoughts of dictating were gone. Coming out of Mobridge they were obliged to back the car up a muddy hill out of the Missouri valley on a crumbling road. An unmarked road cost them two miles; misdirection around a slough cost them more until they drove right through it. The crowds that came out to watch were a mixed blessing. They certainly served to publicize the Trail, but they crowded the car, especially during pit stops.

Dr. Joseph Trotzig, grandson of Joe Parmley, recalls a family story of his grandmother standing out on the Yellowstone Trail with a container of coffee to throw to Joe when he whizzed through Ipswich. She threw, and missed, apparently hitting the side of the car and splattering coffee everywhere.

Still, they made it to Big Stone City in 16 hours and 15 minutes, only 15 minutes late and certainly a record. They were positive they could have made it well within the 16 hours were it not for the foul weather. In spite of the mud, to Parmley, the trip was a success because it showed him faults with the marking of the Trail, and "that the Trail is a great highway and that it is really all that has been said of it "

And the Studebaker? It performed well, needed no repair and did not get scuffed up. It got a bath to remove the 800 pounds of encrusted mud, and was driven back to Aberdeen the next day by another driver since

White canvas covered car in front of Parmley's Land Office ready for the South Dakota run.   Dacotah Prairie Museum, Aberdeen, South Dakota

Mr. Payne was "stiff and sore" from his 16 hours behind the wheel. The Studebaker was immediately sold to an observer of the race.

As amazing as that race was, a more amazing feat was to be performed 31 days later.

Chicago to Seattle in 97 Hours - June 15th, 1915

To dedicate the extended Yellowstone Trail and gain national publicity by proving that a route of this length did exist, the Association conducted a speed and road test. A relay of 21 automobiles carrying a message from Mayor Thompson of Chicago to Mayor Gill of Seattle would try to cover 2445 miles in 100 hours. Could they do it? The fastest train schedule was 70 hours. The auto route was largely over dirt roads that were mere cow paths three years before. The first car left Chicago at noon, June 15th "starting one of the greatest automobile feats ever attempted by this country."[11] The distance was divided into approximately 100 mile segments, the cars running continuously day and night.

Newspapers along the route trumpeted the coming event, encouraging people to come out at the expected times to view their local relay car set off. Extensive encomiums poured from the press, telling the world that a new epoch was starting in cross country travel.

They did it in 97 hours and 10 minutes. Two hours and 50 minutes ahead of schedule! And without a serious accident.

Parmley's report of his ride from Chicago to Stevens Point, Wisconsin to the *Aberdeen American*, in part, follows:

Pictures and press conference were finished and on June 15, 1915 at high twelve [noon] the long journey started with driver D. Boone in a Moline-Knight auto. He bore the letter and a banner which read "Chicago to Seattle over the Yellowstone Trail in 100 hours." He also bore several riders . . . including the president. [In reporting his activities, Parmley always referred to himself in the third person, a literary fashion of the day.] J.R. Edwards of the [Automobile] Blue Book [the preeminent road guide] was also aboard. In a separate car were other Blue Book representatives who would serve as guides as far as Fort Sheridan [Illinois].

Along the beautiful boulevards of Lincoln Park we flew . . . our banner streaming in the wind telling a wondering people that it would be on Puget Sound in 100 hours. We soon saw that we were followed by a motorcycle policeman and the jig was up. I said to Boone, "Turn on the juice and let him know he has to go some if he arrests us." Up went the speedometer to 40, 45, 50 but the police gained. Boone said, "Show him your banner." As he closed up on us I did so and shouted, "We have right of way." He shot by smiling and shouted, "Follow me." He was a special police detailed to escort us out of the city. We followed him and at times he followed us.

Evanston, Highland Park, Winnetka and a numberless lot of suburbs woke out of prosy existence to see us shoot by. Sheridan Road is one of extremes - and if there is any more neglected, forlorn, hopeless, utterly abandoned highway than parts of Sheridan Road as you near the Wisconsin line, will the reader kindly let me know. I would like to study it from an aeroplane.

We rolled into Milwaukee 65 minutes ahead of schedule. The next car, a Maxwell, was waiting and we swept out. Two tires had to be replaced due to blow outs and we lost 35 minutes and finally drafted another car at Fond du Lac as Mr. Rowan, our trailer [emergency car following each relay car] never appeared. As we ran our meteoric course, farmers with their wives and numerous offspring lined the way.

Oshkosh has recently blazed the trail on every fourth pole and every telephone pole on both sides of the street through the city. And they were all out to greet the association's president. Eight thousand people were out. While police held the people back we jumped from one car into another, a Cadillac eight cylinder which bore us through the only really sensational part of over 300 miles on the third relay from Oshkosh to Stevens Point. The small towns were out in force and as darkness came on, bonfires lit up the way. Weyawega surpassed all others - a mile of torches and red fire with a background of men, women and children made a sight seldom seen as our swiftly-moving car went through the cheering files of people.

Don't take the outside seat in going over a sandy road when you have as companions men who delight in talking about their weight. Such conversation adds to your agony. The sandiest stretch from Plymouth Rock to Puget Sound must be near Stevens Point. It was after 20 miles of this that I emerged half paralyzed from a three-inch space in the rear seat of that eight-cylinder Cadillac. I emerged so slowly that I didn't see Andrae and his mechanic shoot by in a 70 horsepower Hope-Hartford sports car with room for only two, bearing the letter and the banner to Chippewa Falls. I was disappointed. I had wanted to stay with the star ship to Aberdeen.[12]

Newspapers, tales of local Trailmen, drivers and a public relations release from the Association continued the commentary, several reflecting on the effects of the rain which had passed over 1500 of the 2500 miles of the route just before the run.

Between Bird Island and Hector, Minnesota, a run-in with a farmer's rig temporarily disabled the relay car, and considerable time was lost in waiting for another car to be sent out from Hector.[13] Seems like another case of a missing trailer car.

A public relations release from the Association continued:

In the hurry of transferring across the Missouri River at Mobridge, the banner was left on the ferry. It was put on the fast coast train to be taken off at Marmarth if the relay car had not left, but the train schedule was too slow and the banner continued on to Miles City. Failing to overtake the relay there, a transfer was made to the Northern Pacific, hoping to pass the car before reaching Billings. Failing to do this, it was continued on the same train to Butte, but Barker was over the crest of the continent, going from Butte to Missoula in an hour and forty minutes faster than any previous record. The last hope was Spokane, and the letter was still ahead. The only thing to do was to continue the banner by express to its destination - the Automobile Club of Seattle. We felt sore at first over this break, but as the letter conveyed by human hands in automobiles traveling on earth roads kept outdistancing the fastest trains on steel tracks, we perked up a little and concluded that our trail wasn't so bad after all."[14]

Parmley continues:

Just to show what some were up against I cite the case of J.W. Harris who had what is looked upon as the hardest run - through the Standing Rock Indian Reservation in the night. He averaged 29.5 miles per hour. The trailer [emergency auto] failed to accompany him and he lost 50 minutes in a washout near McIntosh and was, farther on, so helplessly stuck in a mud hole with no help that he walked and ran to McLaughlin, three miles, got two automobiles to go back and pull his car out. This took two hours and ten minutes. All this in the dead of a cloudy night.[15]

Another reported of "being stuck in muddy ruts near 'Pease Bottom' at Hysham, Montana and still setting a speed record of 27.6 miles per hour between Miles City and Billings.[16]

And then there was Walter Beck who was to drive from Missoula to Wallace, Idaho. He had just begun his ride and was a short distance west of Missoula when he was forced to stop because of a broken wheel. The Reo car which was trailing Beck took the letter and raced on to Wallace, arriving two hours ahead of schedule. Meanwhile, Beck, wishing to keep

Yellowstone Trail Association medallion/watch fob used as part of the campaign to have cars allowed in Yellowstone National Park

the spirit of the relay, completed his run with a new wheel that had been rushed from Missoula. [17]

One mystified Trail booster later wrote, "Why go to all this trouble when you can send the d—d letter for two cents."[18] But trouble they took, and they achieved their goal which was to see if they could do it. And they did it with almost three hours to spare. Parmley summed up the superb organizational effort in a speech two years later, saying with his dry wit, "We hurried some."[19]

Opening Yellowstone National Park to the Auto - August 1, 1915
"For the Enjoyment of the American People"

By 1915 Yellowstone Park was the only national park denying autos. It is reasonable that a road organization formed to enable the auto tourist to get to the Yellowstone National Park would work toward opening the park to autos. The Association joined the many voices raised in the cause and, among other things, issued a medallion. But just the fact that the Yellowstone Trail was attracting autoists to the Park in burgeoning numbers increased the urgency of the question of admission.

In 1912 the U.S. Senate asked for cost estimates to compare improving and broadening the present roads designed for horse carriage trams for auto use to the cost of developing a second road system for autos alone. At the time, the national parks were under the jurisdiction of the War Department. Acting Secretary of War Robert S. Oliver investigated, even surveyed engineers and travelers, and concluded that one single, broadened road system would be more economical to build and maintain, but still an entrance fee "of a couple of dollars" would now have to be charged.[20] Even rebuilding one road to support autos would cost about $2,500,000 and yearly maintenance would run $100,000. His investigation into cost caused Oliver to refuse to permit autos to enter. Even a letter from the governor of Colorado to President Taft could not budge thinking on the matter.

Park concessionaires, such as the horse-drawn omnibus operators and the hotel operators, supported the ban on autos. They preferred to cater to the rich who arrived by train, stayed in hotels and hired tour carriages. Automobiles would introduce an element of society who could see the wonders of nature on their own, without a guide, and who could bring their own camping gear rather than stay in one of Wylie Company's permanent, elegant tents. There would be noise, and one must consider the health of the 1400 working horses in the park. Besides, they said, the roads were

Cars at Yellowstone National Park north (Gardiner) entrance. 1924
Western Magazine

not wide enough to accommodate both horses and horseless carriages. Of course, loss of revenue and the cost of the motor omnibuses was their main grief, but that went unsaid. Keeping visitors immobile controlled them.

Oliver's report included consideration of entrance roads: "The northern approach road is the most important road in the park as it gives access to the headquarters of the park and to the Army post of Fort Yellowstone located near park headquarters and must be kept open for traffic in the winter. . . . In providing for use of automobiles on the present roads, the northern and western approach roads and certain side roads . . . should be developed."[21] The northern entrance was the one served by the Yellowstone Trail.

As a result of further study and enormous motoring public pressure, Oliver finally acquiesced. At last in April 1915 Secretary of Interior Franklin K. Lane announced that automobiles would be allowed in beginning August 1. The fee was either $5 or $10, depending upon the number of seats in the car. There were no garages in the park, so the automobilist was required to prove that he carried enough gas and spare parts and that his brakes were good enough to skid to a stop. Rules were handed out warning drivers to always defer to horse-drawn vehicles, never overtake them, and to stay 150 yards away from everything. All traffic moved one way, the autos leaving one half hour before the horse-drawn vehicles and adhering to a strict time schedule. The schedules were given to visitors and checking stations were manned by park guards to make sure no one speeded beyond their schedule. The purpose of these rules "is to subject the automobile tourists to the least number of restrictions . . ."[22]

Among the many requests for copies of the automobile rules was one from J.W. Parmley dated July 20, 1915.

Other Trails and Their Sponsoring Organizations

The Yellowstone Trail was not the only long-distance route during this period. There is little indication of communication among the trail/highway organizations, and information about the others' methods and accomplishments apparently was passed primarily by news articles in auto-related and popular journals.

In 1912, the year the Yellowstone Trail came to life, the National Old Trails Road Ocean-to-Ocean Highway Association was formed to create a route along the old National Road and, to the west, selected pre-auto trails such as the Santa Fe. That same year A.L. Westgard, a "pathfinder" for AAA, made three cross-country trips, naming one path the Northwest Trail, another the Overland Trail, and a third the Midland Trail. These three trails, however, had no active sponsoring group to promote and maintain them.

Other sponsored trails followed quickly, including the Lincoln Highway begun in 1913 from New York to San Francisco, the Jefferson Highway from Winnipeg to New Orleans, the Park-to-Park Highway connecting eight national parks in the West, the William Penn Highway across Pennsylvania, and the Columbia River Highway. By 1920 the Dixie Highway from Chicago to Miami and the Bankhead Highway, named after the author of the 1916 federal

Yellowstone Trail Near Yellowstone National Park north (Gardiner) entrance. Yellowstone National Park Archives

The Literary Digest for May 26, 1923 listed these four coast to coast highways as the most important.

aid bill, from San Diego to Washington, D.C. were in existence. Soon a myriad of trails could be found, 250 of which were chronicled by the AAA. And probably there were many more short, intrastate trails. By the middle 1920's the traveler was faced with a confusion of painted symbols along the popular roads. Road junctions were a veritable jumble of colors. It was so bad around the Lake Erie area that when the Yellowstone Trail Association applied to add their symbol to the plethora of route markers, their petition was rejected in 1915 and the Trail took a more southern route throough New York and Connecticut. By 1919, however, the Association had somehow found a way to move its route through the desired area.

Sponsored Trails Had Detractors

Throughout the time of the building of the Yellowstone Trail many local chapters of the Good Roads Association worked amicably with the myriad small trail organizations that were springing up all over the country. However, not everyone thought privately organized and run Trails was the way to go. In Wisconsin, for instance, the secretary of the Good Roads Association, Frank Cannon, forcefully voiced many anti-trail arguments. Cannon felt that trail organizations were only "travel agencies," had no constructive plans to offer for road improvement, did not work for state highway roads but just for "their" road, and begged for money. He wanted trail organizations to spend their time working for good highways rather than "marking indifferent roads."[23]   He was convinced that a legislative approach to the development of state trunk lines was the way to build good highways and that the Trail Associations' county-by-county approach would not work. His negative view of trail organizations may have been formed from the many short, and short lived, trails which started with much huzza but had no organized follow-up or maintenance, leaving a string of bad roads and unhappy subscribers. His diatribes against all trail organizations in general, and the Yellowstone Trail in particular, continued from about 1917 until 1920 from his pulpit, the Good Roads for Wisconsin magazine.[24]

His attack on questionable actions of many trail organizations was well warranted, but his own bias toward simply creating state built and maintained roads made him blind to the possible good that could come from the broader goals of some trail associations.

Trail associations, especially the Yellowstone Trail Association, did indeed have broader interests. They sought good roads, but they sought good roads specifically to support economic development and tourism along their route. They believed that motivating heavy traffic along a road stimulated appropriate rebuilding and improvement of that route. And indeed, towns and counties along the Yellowstone Trail did dedicate more resources to the Trail simply because the need became obvious. In fact, the first cross-state route in Wisconsin to be completely paved was the Yellowstone Trail, simply because the traffic created by the Association warranted the expense.

The Trail Had Grown Up

From that first meeting in April, 1912 through the year 1915, the Yellowstone Trail Association and the Trail itself had done a lot of growing up. The Trail was now in existence from Chicago to Seattle. The initial five officers were now joined by an increasing number of staff to raise money and superintend the route. With a limited budget of membership fees, they took credit for getting $1 million spent on roads by counties along the Trail in 1913 and 1914. They also took pains to engender national thinking about the Trail. What happened to the Trail in Minneapolis or Marmarth affected all on the Trail. If there was a need in any spot, it became a need for all to attend to it.

Ambition seemed to outrun reality for the members of the Yellowstone Trail Association. But maybe that was a key to what made the founders and members tick. They did push imagination and energy to outer bounds. They were practical imaginers. It was their energy, perseverance and foresight which was making the four purposes unfold: creating a transcontinental road, attracting funds, attracting tourists, and perpetuating the integrity of their vision of a national network of roads.

Endnotes

1. Aberdeen News Feb.15, 1913:1.
2. Adams County Record May 14, 1914:1.
3. Adams County Record May 28, 1914:1.
4. Adams County Record June 4, 1914:1.
5. Minutes of the Second Annual Meeting of the National Parks Highway Association March 29, 1916:1 (Eastern Washington University Archives, Cheney, Washington, Box 2, File 2:32.)
6. Ismay Journal March 5, 1915.
7. Aberdeen Daily News February 6, 1915.
8. Minutes of the Second Annual Meeting of National Parks Highway Association March 29, 1916:1   (Eastern Washington University Archives, Cheney, Washington Box 2 File 2:32.)
9. Douglas Shelor, manager of the Automobile Club of Western Washington, quoted in Western Highways Builder 20 (Nov. 1920) 23.
10. Aberdeen Daily News May 17, 1915.
11. Mineral Independent June 24, 1915.
12. Aberdeen American June (no date) 1915.
13. Olivia Times June 17, 1915.
14. Yellowstone Trail Association public relations release June 19, 1915. (South Dakota State Historical Society Archives, Beebe Papers.)
15. Ibid.
16. Warren R. McGee, "Yellowstone Trail Data" unpublished, typed 9 page script. 1977 (Montana State University-Bozeman. Burlingame Special Collection file 1204 Yellowstone Trail 1911-1935.)
17. Mineral Independent June 24, 1915.
18. Yellowstone Trail Association public relations release June 19, 1915. (South Dakota State Historical Society Archives Beebe Papers.)
19. Joseph Parmley Speech in Oshkosh, Wisconsin January 18, 1917. (South Dakota State Historical Society Archives, Parmley Papers, SC 10, folder #4, Yellowstone Highway Association Records 1914-1939.)
20. Senate Document #871, 62nd Congress July 1, 1912. (Washington, D.C: US Government Printing Office 1912) 8.
21. Ibid.
22. Secretary of the Interior Franklin K. Lane press release, Letter Box #22 "Automobiles 1915" Item #44 Yellowstone National Park Archives.
23 Good Roads for Wisconsin January 1917:8.
24. q.v. Good Roads for Wisconsin January 1917, April 1918, August 1919, and November 1920.

Chapter Three

1916 - 1920   The Formative Years

A friend of the authors' recalls, as a child, riding with her family on the Trail from Seattle to the Midwest: "Going over the mountains in Idaho was the worst. We had to tie a log to the back of the car to slow us going down hill. But that's the way you traveled then - creatively."

To grow and prosper, the Yellowstone Trail Association also had to think creatively.

The formative years of the Yellowstone Trail Association, 1916-1920, spanned the turmoil of World War I, the national rethinking of road financing and responsibility, considerable maturing of the automobile and the beginning of the great era of long distance automobile touring. The Yellowstone Trail Association accepted the challenges and became a strong national organization.

The Federal-Aid Road Act of 1916

A giant step forward in the battle for funds to build connected roads was taken with the Federal Aid Road Act of 1916. The Act began the modern policy of providing federal aid money to states for construction of rural post roads, although the provision was so broad as to enable almost any rural road to qualify. It would apportion $75 million to states according to a formula based on population, post road mileage and area. The federal government would provide 30%-50% of the cost and the state would provide the remainder. To qualify, states must have established a highway department which would designate a limited system to which it would confine its federal aid. That is, the Act "was designated to coordinate the main intersection roads in the same manner that the previous road laws had integrated the county road systems."[1] Roads ending at the border of one state had not necessarily met up with a road in the next state. This Act worked to ensure a meeting. The policy that the Yellowstone Trail Association and others had sought of coordinating main roads finally had arrived. The law was the first comprehensive act of the national government aimed at the establishment of a nationwide system of interstate highways. The law recognized the sovereignty of states to select the method of construction and maintenance of the roads, as long as they had the prospect of being a through road.

Western papers saw the Act as a godsend and the opportunity to be finally pulled out of the mud.

Developing the Routing of the Yellowstone Trail

The task of routing had to continue. In a compelling paean to the Trail, J.W. Parmley outlined his criteria for routing the Trail: "In determining a route that is going to be a transcontinental highway, many elements must be considered such as the fertility of the soil, future possible productivity, past and present road conditions, resourcefulness and development of the country, connections with other highways, scenery, and above all the intelligence and enterprise of the people along the way."[2] J.W. Parmley always felt that the route he had in mind was a "natural route" from Aberdeen to the Yellowstone National Park because the scenery was magnificent, it was the most direct of any automobile road from the Twin Cities to the Park, and it ran along part of the Lewis and Clark route near the Yellowstone River.

Young cities had sprung up along the Milwaukee Road railroad route that the Trail usually paralleled in the West, affording shelter and services to weary travelers. That he was thinking of an eventual route crossing the country was a surety. He had mentioned to many this "dream" of a country criss-crossed with transcontinental roads. Some called him just that, a dreamer, and dismissed him as such. Others saw his vision as practical, though distant, given state and national reticence to invest in roads, especially paved highways.

Building auto roads next to rail lines was not new. Stewart explains that
"Roads tended to follow a railroad because a railroad itself
was also the shortest line between two towns and because towns
were strung out along the track. Moreover, the right-of-way for
a road could be established alongside the railroad with minimal
disturbance to farms and private holdings. Also, the roads may have
followed the railroads for safety. If you bogged down hopelessly
in the gumbo or broke an axle, a freight train or a handcar might
be prevailed upon to stop and take the wife and children into the
next town."[3]

A headline in the *Aberdeen Daily American* gives some idea of the competitive spirit of communities vying for the Trail. It declared triumphantly "South Dakota Wins Out Over Northern Pacific: Trail Assured Aberdeen."[4] Aberdeen was on the Milwaukee Road line.

There had been apparently quite a battle between advocates of the Trail following the Great Northern Railroad through North Dakota and central Montana, and advocates of the Milwaukee Road route. The Milwaukee Road adherents prevailed, and the route from the Twin Cities to the Yellowstone Park did follow that railroad into Montana.

The choice of the Milwaukee Road by the Yellowstone Trail Association left a bad feeling within the community of Glendive, Montana, 72 miles northeast of Miles City and on the Great Northern Railroad line. If the Trail followed the Milwaukee Road, Glendive would not be included. After the first annual convention closed, a news item appeared in a Glendive paper showing this bitter feeling:

> Those Miles City business men would better quit flirting with the Yellowstone Trail Association, which is vainly seeking to bring the transcontinental automobile trail into Montana along the Milwaukee [Road] right of way, and get in line with Glendive on this proposition. If Miles is ever on that route, it will only be when the road comes through Glendive, either directly from Dickinson [North Dakota], or else branching off from the Great Northern right of way at Mondak . . . it behooves all Northern Pacific points to work together. The road will assuredly never enter Montana via Ismay and Baker.[5]

Yellowstone Trail under improvement along the Milwaukee Road.
First Year Book of the Twin Cities-Aberdeen-Yellowstone Park Trail 1914

But the road did, assuredly, enter Montana via Baker and Ismay, and thence to Terry and Miles City. The region around these towns was semi-arid, sparsely populated and had few established roads. A tentative and tortured route was selected following the Milwaukee Road Railway which did a brisk business in shipping cattle from Ismay.

Enlisting the financial support of communities along the Trail became paramount to achieve the financial wherewithal to succeed in this endeavor. However, getting joiners would not be a problem if the route was located along a railway. It seemed that everyone wanted the Trail to be routed through their community to reap the benefits of fame, fortune, and tourists. Many little towns along the railroad, such as Webster, South Dakota and Ortonville, Minnesota, showed up at the Miles City first annual convention armed with letters pledging support from the business community, and promising to host good roads meetings and whatever else was needed.

An essential structural component of the Association for establishing local roads to comprise the great route was the "locating committee." Community-based locating committees were charged with locating already-existing local roads which would be the best route to the next community's choice of road. If no convenient road existed, local members of the Yellowstone Trail Association or the Trailman would see it their duty to influence county officials to spend tax dollars to build one. Maps of these locations, along with local landform and geologic descriptions, were forwarded to the Yellowstone Trail Association executive committee. Unfortunately, in some cases where no roads existed, mere wagon trails were chosen, causing bad publicity for the organization.

Since the Association was not actually building the roads, it had no choice but to commit to a policy of leaving the final selection of specific roads to the choice of local or county organizations with expert county advice. However, the Executive Committee reserved the right to route the Trail in general to keep it near the Milwaukee Road and to keep it the shortest route to the Yellowstone Park.

In order for the entire Trail to be built as closely to a single standard as possible, the Association formed a "committee on specifications in 1914. They recommended:

1. A grade of not less than 20 feet wide be made with elevating or other road grader.

2. The crown of said grade be not less than 1 ft. above the original sod.

3. There be a gradual slope from the crown to the side ditches distant 22 feet from center.

4. Where higher grades are necessary the slope thereof be such that

there will be no possibility of vehicles tipping over.

5. In grading sloughs, material should be brought from higher ground.

6. That all stones be removed from the 66 foot highway [*right of way*].

7. That at all times drainage be provided for.

8. A system of road control be inaugurated; one man with split log drag working half time can maintain 10 miles of dirt or gravel road.

9. That graveling be done as soon as possible and that the higher type of road be made of concrete.

10. At every town and section corner a sign be placed giving distance and direction to the next town.

11. So far as possible, these signs should be painted on large boulders with chrome yellow with black lettering thereon.

12. Barring engineering problems, a route as short and straight as possible be selected, in view of the fact that the route is going to be a great national highway. [6]

These recommendations were addressed to the membership at large, presumably with the hope that they would be carried to county boards. This approach gave credibility to the local Yellowstone Trail people as they worked with the county to select and maintain the best standard route.

Splendid Laterals

Since many communities wanted "in" on the Trail, the Trail Association was often faced with problems of balancing a short, straight route to the Yellowstone National Park against entreaties of loyal boosters from divergent communities. A compromise of sorts was reached for a brief time in the form of "splendid laterals," spurs that extended from the Trail. There were 23 such laterals in 1914, but it appears that they were included only to placate those active communities. They served as "collector" roads, but the Association had no intention of diffusing the Trail resources to include them. One lateral, for instance, ran from the Twin Cities to Duluth, Minnesota; another ran from Pompey's Pillar in Montana to the Custer Battlefield. The Yellowstone Trail Association did not recognize the claims of these communities who advertised themselves as "being on the Yellowstone Trail."

This apparently proved awkward in the case of John Gibson, a strong supporter of the organization and a manufacturer of reinforced concrete culverts. Unfortunately, he lived in Fromberg, Montana, about 15 miles south of the Trail community of Park City, Montana. Yellowstone Trail Association maps of Montana at the time show, in small print at the bottom, "Gibson Culvert used in constructing this road." He got his advertising, but he didn't get Trail Association recognition for Fromberg. In only one instance did the Association produce a map with the lateral labeled as the Yellowstone Trail. The map showed a line dropping south from the Trail at Laurel, Montana, running through Gibson's Fromberg and then to Cody, Wyoming and turning west to enter the Yellowstone Park. This map appeared on page 5 of the *First Year Book of the Twin Cities-Aberdeen-Yellowstone Park Trail 1914* and, written in very small print right on that line is, "Home of Gibson Concrete Culvert Company" with a tiny arrow pointing to Fromberg.[7] There was no other such advertising on that or any other map produced by the Yellowstone Trail Association. Hotel, restaurant and garage ads appeared, but along edges of maps or as pages in a separate guide. The authors can only conclude that Gibson influenced some unknown person for that single appearance of the splendid lateral containing the tiny arrow showing his town. It probably vastly upset the Trail founders. An eastern entrance to the Park was never entertained because it was not the best route.

The only lateral actively maintained by the Association ran from Livingston, Montana to the north entrance of Yellowstone Park because that was the nearest entrance for tourists who followed the Yellowstone Trail. That lateral also ran parallel with the Northern Pacific Railroad Park Branch.

There were many opportunities for branch roads, but the organization acted to limit such diffusion and to direct its energies toward maintaining an east-west road. Accusations that the organization would run the road to any community that wanted "in" and which would pay the fee were unwarranted, because the published aim of the organization was to create the shortest interstate route to Yellowstone Park. At no time did the Association reroute the Trail from a community due to non-payment of fees. They threatened at times, but never did it. Stevens Point, Wisconsin became three years behind in dues, but did not lose the Trail to a nearby town which even offered to pay Stevens Point's arrears as inducement for inclusion. That town lay south and would not have been on "the shortest route."

In 1915, in preparation for the extension from Chicago to Plymouth Rock that the Association had voted for the previous year, Vice President M.J. Dowling was dispatched to investigate a possible route. He was prevented from following Lake Erie closely because there were already so many other shorter trails with their signs and colors that no more permits were issued in Ohio or in Massachusetts. A more southern route was temporarily chosen.

While anyone can connect the dots on a map of the United States with a broad pen and declare the route laid or "done," it is a different matter to draw each of the little county roads recommended by local "locating committees" on even enlarged maps, especially if the roads followed the township survey lines. Since the 1785 Land Ordinance, all of the land in the United States generally to the west of a line through Ohio has been surveyed on the "rectangular survey system." One mile square sections of land were laid out all over federally owned land, initially all Western land. Each section consisted of 640 acres and often sold in units of a quarter section or 160 acres. Sixty-six feet of land between sections was reserved for public right-of-way. As a result, there tended to be right angle turns or intersections every mile. The maps in the *First Year Book of the Twin Cities-Aberdeen-Yellowstone Park Trail 1914* amply illustrate the product. The solution to this problem can still be seen today; hundreds of rounded off corners can be found in the western states, sometimes with old picnic areas between the new curved corner and the old square corner.

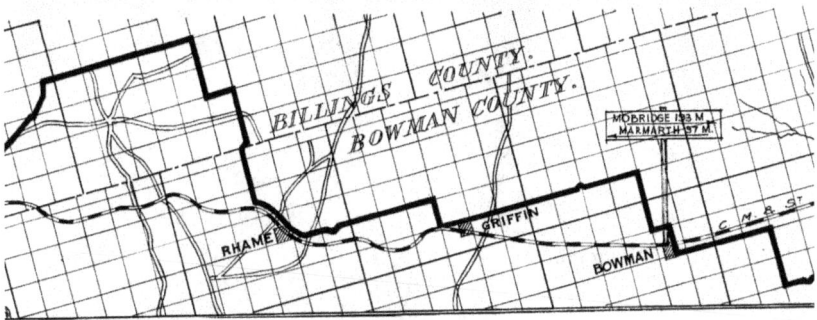

Marking the Trail

When the Trail Association was first formed, the color chosen to splash on telegraph poles, rocks, and anything else along the Trail, was, naturally, yellow, chrome yellow. It appeared as yellow bands in some states, and a yellow blob elsewhere. In 1914 the group selected a uniform symbol which appeared on all stationery, literature, advertisements and road signs. [See next page.] It consisted of a yellow circle with a black arrow in the center pointing toward the Yellowstone Park. Metal road signs were designed and fastened to posts, but paint was still daubed on rocks and poles, when handy. In White Butte, South Dakota, natural hoodoo sand pillars found in the "badland" area nearby did duty. Recently, a small cast iron Yellowstone Trail sign was found in Montana.

For the most part, the people who marked the Trail and re-marked it as needed were local Trailmen, but college students were also hired for the summers. One of the most avid markers was General Manager H.O. Cooley's son, Parle. It must have been a thankless task, because there were complications in receiving the metal signs and gallons of chrome yellow paint at the right place at the right time when shipped by train. Also, the finances of the organization were always perilous, and the young men were expected to collect their expenses from towns along the Trail. The work was outdoors, rain or shine, and housing was not always available.

From Ohio east the Trail was less well marked because the Trail Association lacked the tight organization it possessed in the west. Also, the eastern route changed about 1919, [see map p.vi] and there was great competition for space on poles.

From Plymouth Rock to Seattle in 121 hours - September 1916

Without a doubt, the main event of 1916 for the Yellowstone Trail Association was the September run from Plymouth Rock to Seattle. In

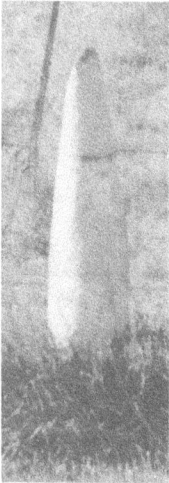

Metal marker

Photos by authors

Left. Hoodoo marker with yellow stripe.

Yellowstone Trail sign on garage, probably at Miles City, Montana. Photo by Garry Schye.

Left. White Butte, SD hoodoo used as Trail marker.
First Year Book of the Twin Cities-Aberdeen-Yellowstone Park Trail 1914

Right. Trail marker near Snoqualmie Pass, WA.
Photo by authors.

February the Association convention had approved the extension of the Trail from Chicago to Plymouth Rock and a route had been tentatively selected. "Desirous of demonstrating farther the superiority of the Yellowstone Trail, the Association challenged the Lincoln Highway Association to an ocean to ocean race. The disability [disadvantage] of the Yellowstone Trail was more than 400 miles. The challenge was not accepted."[8] The Lincoln Highway Association had already made a coast-to-coast run in 138.5 hours over 3384 miles, averaging 24.4 miles per hour from New York to San Francisco.[9] Anxious to beat that record and to test the route even without the Lincoln Highway people competing, Parmley promised a run of 3673 miles in 120 hours at an average speed of 31 miles per hour.

The run also had the potential to cement interest in the Trail as a unit, and to advertise its possible use in civil defense. World War I had been raging in Europe for two years and in about seven months the United States would be dragged into it; transcontinental roads were now seen as a military necessity. Parmley asked the War Department if it was interested in the experiment of running a message from Plymouth to Seattle. The Army was interested and readily agreed to dispatch a message over the Trail, making it an official test of military and civilian organization. The organizational machinery of the Association geared up.

The run was planned in 14 relays with a manager for each relay of 100-400 mile segments. The manager could subdivide his relay into 50 to 150-mile segments. As a result, 64 autos carried the Army message in the relay. Add 126 "trailer" cars for emergency, and a total of 190 cars participated. The race began under the panoply covering the historic rock at Plymouth, Massachusetts at noon September 11 when Colonel W.E. Craighill delivered a sealed message to Robert Harlow who was waiting in a big Packard Twin Six with engine throbbing. The town clock began to strike twelve when the Packard was off. And they made the run in 121 hours and 12 minutes - 72 minutes more than their announced 120 hours. Jim Parsons in a Stutz dashed into Fort Lawton, Seattle, and handed the letter to Captain H.W. Bunn at 10:12 A.M. September 16. They might have made it early if not for 600 miles and 24 hours of continuous rain and hail across Wisconsin and Minnesota and a cloudburst in South Dakota. They also lost time in the Cascade Mountains of Washington.[10] The official time was published as 30.3 miles per hour for the approximately 3670 miles.

Local papers described the daring-do of local drivers using such phrases as "reckless abandon," and "better than 40 miles an hour" and describing one car as "stripped of its windshield, top and fenders and with the body of the car strapped down to the axles." "Leaving but a streak of dust" was a favorite of reporters, and once a viewer was quoted as saying the driver was driving "like a bat out of h—l." There were no accidents, but break adjustments and flat tires seemed to be common. A close call occurred near Superior, Montana: " . . . on a downgrade he had to run the car into a gravel bank, the brakes stopping it in about its length, to avoid a collision with an elderly woman who was driving by team up the road. She did not know about the relay. She had come in from a side road and was not seen by the road patrollers" [who kept the road clear for the relay]. Careful time was kept by the locals, recording down to the second when one car stopped and the next began. There was much crowing about being ahead of schedule. Montana was rightfully proud because the message arrived in Montana one hour late and left the Treasure State two hours ahead of time. A remarkable 34 miles per hour was maintained.[11]

Excessive praise once again appeared in newspapers, heralding the Yellowstone Trail as the great Northwest route, the best route to the playground of the three National Parks (Yellowstone, Glacier, and Mt. Rainier), and a scenic route with no deserts. The Association bragged that, "we made the fastest time ever made by automobile across the continent and demonstrated the superiority of the Yellowstone Trail over every other highway as to its organization, the road itself, and the sportsmanlike spirit of its sponsors."[12]

The Yellowstone Trail Goes to War - 1917

The Great War taught Americans many lessons about the importance of roads in war time and about the failings of American roads. While taxis and private automobiles were shuttling soldiers to battlefields and to hospitals in France, a feat possible only because of good roads, Americans were bogged down in quagmires, unable to transport matériel to eastern ports from the middle west. If "necessity is the mother of invention" then the United States was the benefactor of this necessity. The military forced the creation of strategic road links and it forced sleepy states into a recognition of their road inadequacy.

Only nine months had passed between the passage of the 1916 Federal Aid Road Act and America's entrance into World War I, hardly time enough for any improvement to have been enacted. Rail congestion of major proportions resulted in the government seizure of railroads in late 1917. Railways were sinking into lethargy just as auto use was dramatically rising. The military ceased shipping trucks from Detroit to points of embarkation by rail and began driving them. This was a new concept of mobility. The inadequacy of the American road system was soon apparent in the unprecedented outpouring of trucks onto roads incapable of carrying the heavy weight. Only 11.3% of the whole highway system of 2,451,660 miles was surfaced by 1917.[13] The inability to obtain steel to repair bridges during the war magnified the problem. Ruts, snow and mud delayed these motorized wagon trains, and traffic jammed on inadequate roads and near seaports.

The rail congestion also affected farmers, forcing them to find other ways of reaching the market. New England manufacturing cities were forced to use trucks instead of rails to make shipments. The war opened our eyes to the possibility of long-distance truck transport as well as local trucking. For-hire trucking flourished as commercial companies saw the savings of door-to-door transport and short hauls over drayage to and from railroad stations. By the end of 1918 there were 525,000 non-military trucks of all sizes plying their trade.[14]

When the war broke out, use of asphalt, oil and tar products in our country ran into the hundreds of millions of gallons. These products were withdrawn from highway and street work during the war. Non-military roads would have to wait their turn.

The advent of the war only magnified for the American people the need for good roads, a truth the Yellowstone Trail Association had been preaching for five years. The war years did not change the mission of the Association and it carried on, holding its 1917 and 1918 meetings as planned. The Association did not, however, publish the 1918 version of their popular and useful Route Folder which had in previous years contained mileages and services in towns along the route. In 1918 the headquarters of the Association was moved from Aberdeen to Minneapolis, and the organization was incorporated.

In 1917 more than $3 million in road improvements were expected along the Trail. That figure dropped to $2.5 million in 1918 in spite of the Trail being designated as a military road. Between 1917 and 1919, 110 miles of Trail were hard-surfaced, 160 miles rose from the level of dirt to gravel, and one bridge was built. In spite of rubber tire and gas shortages, people still traveled the Trail, 6440 auto parties traveling 1100 miles or more, according to Trail registrations at the Mobridge bureau in 1918, up from 4129 in 1916.[15]

At the end of the war, the U.S. government became the largest owner of trucks in the world. The Secretaries of War and of Agriculture were given the job of distributing 22,710 surplus vehicles. State governments had only to request them and pay transportation fees. This was a windfall to road construction. A veritable explosion of road building desires occurred in 1919 because of the windfall of trucks, unexpended funds from the 1916 Act and a new knowledge of the importance of roads. Local bond issues were passed in unprecedented numbers to improve roads.

An interesting addendum to the tale of the Army and roads concerns a young Captain Dwight D. Eisenhower who participated in what was dubbed the "first transcontinental motor convoy" in 1919. General Pershing wished to demonstrate the importance of truck transport during times of war, and to demonstrate how unprepared our roads were to support truck traffic. To that end about 80 vehicles, 260 enlisted men and 35 officers traveled from

Offices of the Association were in rooms on the second floor of this still existing Aberdeen building during 1917-1918. Photo by authors.

Washington, D.C. to San Francisco along the Lincoln Highway. Fifty-six days and 1,900 breakdowns later they arrived, telling tales of pulling trucks over desert sand by rope, of dust-stalled engines and mud-mired machines.[16] That experience must have been most memorable for the young man, because it would benefit our entire nation 35 years later with the unveiling of the Eisenhower Interstate System.

Association offices were in the Northern States Power building in Minneapolis from 1918-1924. Photo by authors.

Financing the Yellowstone Trail Association

What money did the Association have? The big money needed to pay for highway building lay in township, county and state coffers. Delegates to Trail meetings pledged their county's "cooperation" and "in kind" or relatively small contributions, and individuals donated or volunteered their skills and/or equipment on local levels. The organization costs were supported with small amounts of money raised through subscriptions and memberships. This money was used, as outlined in bylaws, for leadership expenses and for publication of the organization's many maps, brochures and public relations releases, and, of course, yellow paint. Their second purpose as an organization was to push public agencies to provide road-building money. This they accomplished. One exception was the time the Association raised $28,000 for two special road projects. But the organization was not formed as a money-making scheme, and the organization lived up to that end admirably.

Almost every year a new fee structure was constructed, mostly based upon the size of community and membership, but the organization chose to attract a large member base by a small assessment of approximately $5 per member organization and $1 per individual. In 1916 several state meetings of the Yellowstone Trail Association concluded that the income was too small for a national undertaking of that size.

The Association reported that hundreds of thousand and even millions of dollars were spent on the Yellowstone Trail. This was money that they convinced counties to spend on the Trail. The Association never saw the big money. However, without their urging, as they saw it, the roads would not have been built, at least not as quickly. They measured their success at persuasion by counties' dollars. The actual income of the association increased from $90 in 1912 to about $31,200 in 1920.[17] A 1921 report of the group's income shows a growth to $40,000, most of which was used for items that were given away. When the organization dissolved in 1930, the assets were a little less than the debts.

What did the Yellowstone Trail Association Accomplish?

One could argue that without the Association, roads and travel would have developed in just about the same way and at the same pace. Perhaps. It is certainly true that the advent of the automobile and the increasing need and desire for personal transportation were the powering forces for improvement. The Yellowstone Trail, the Lincoln Highway and the other sponsored trails were the logical and effective means to start making those improvements and to

> The Yellowstone Trail is the best organized highway in America. It owes the position that it has occupied among the highways of the country, in its proud place at the top, to two things: First, that it is an undivided route extending across the United States, and it has kept good faith with all the communities through which it passes. Second, it has a continuous and positive organization that works for the whole of the road 365 days of the year.
> *Waconia Patriot*
> *March 29, 1917*

"rally the troops" to urge governments to continue them. The Yellowstone Trail Association, particularly, represented the will of dozens of organizations of businessmen giving them a concerted voice. The Association, by attracting tourists by the thousands with its travel guidance, promoted the economic progress of a large number of communities along the Trail.

America began to view long distance travel as possible for the middle-class. Neither a war nor the influenza epidemic of 1918 nor a drought had stifled a public cry for more room to roam and better roads to roam upon.

Endnotes

1. Albert C. Rose, Historic American Roads: From Frontier Trails to Superhighways (North Dakota: Crown Publishers, 1976) 90.

2. Joseph Parmley Speech in Oshkosh, Wisconsin January 18, 1917. (South Dakota State Historical Society Archives. Parmley Papers Yellowstone Highway Association Records SC 10, folder #4, 1914-1939).

3. George R. Stewart, U.S.: A Cross Section of the United States of America (Westport, Conn: Greenwood Press, Publishers, 1953 reprinted in 1973) 22.

4. Aberdeen Daily American Feb 19, 1913:1.

5. Miles City Independent early 1913 no date available.

6. Adams County Record April 24, 1913:1 and Aberdeen Am. April 18, 1913.

7. O.T. Peterson, The First Year Book of the Twin Cities-Aberdeen-Yellowstone Park Trail (St. Paul: The Pioneer Company, 1914) 5.

8. Joseph Parmley Speech in Oshkosh, Wisconsin January 18, 1917. (South Dakota State Historical Society Archives. Parmley Papers Yellowstone Highway Association Records SC 10, folder #4, 1914-1939).

9. H.O. Cooley, "Story of Transcontinental Auto Run Tells of Every Relay," Northwestern Motorist October 1916:16.

10. Ibid.

11. q.v. Mineral Independent September 21, 1916:1, or Hector (Minnesota) News Mirror September 21, 1916 or H.O. Cooley, "Story of Transcontinental Auto Run Tells of Every Relay" Northwestern Motorist October 1916.

12. Joseph Parmley Speech in Oshkosh, Wisconsin January 18, 1917.

13. Motor Age April 5, 1917.

14. Department of Transportation, America's Highways: 1776-1976. A History of the Federal-Aid Program. (Washington, DC: U.S. Government Printing Office 1976) 98.

15. Yellowstone Trail Association, Yellowstone Trail Association Folder, 1917 and 1919 editions.

16. q.v. Poyntz Tyler, (editor) American Highways Today The Reference Shelf Vol. 29, No. 1. (New York: The H.W. Wilson Co. 1957) 129 or Phil Patton, Open Road: A Celebration of the American Highway (N Y: Simon/Schuster, 1986) 81.

17. Western Tourist October 1921:50.

Chapter Four

1921 - 1925 The Grand Years

The "grand years" saw the Yellowstone Trail recognized across the nation. In 1924 membership was at its highest at 8143. Its financial situation was stable: always slightly in the red. Federal aid had become an accepted concept, with state highway commissions now beginning to link main roads into a sensible interstate web. The marking of the Trail coast-to-coast was standardized and efficiency in operating a national organization was achieved. Emphasis could now be placed on the third purpose of the Association, that of generating tourism on the Trail. This goal was especially stressed in the East where the Association's western founders were too remote to be effective in meeting the other goals.

The "grand years" also witnessed advances in road funding, aids for tourists, and the sport of camping.

Advances in Road Funding

After Congress passed the innovative 1916 Federal Aid bill, it did not pass a renewed highway bill until after January 1, 1921, leaving states frustratingly unsure of any aid. To raise road funds, in the meantime, some states had enacted higher taxes on auto registrations and, following Oregon, implemented a state tax on motor fuel. In addition to extending the 1916 Act for another one-year appropriation, the 1921 legislation included restrictions upon states to concentrate their use of the funds on connecting trunk routes, rather than on a shotgun selection of roads.

The 1916 and 1921 Federal-Aid Acts formed the basis for the present-day road funding relationship between state and federal governments: states would decide routes and perform the work, federal government officials would approve the route and see that certain standards of construction were followed. But the philosophical battle continued between supporters of federally *built* and *maintained* roads vs. the supporters of federal-*aid* to states. T.H. MacDonald, Chief of the Bureau of Public Roads for 34 years, felt that "states must retain the initiative in administering federal-aid highway programs and that his Bureau would only check on them to protect the federal interest."[1]

The Yellowstone Trail Association's position on whether the states or the national government should build roads is not clear in the few remaining papers of the Association. The Association, in 1919, endorsed the Townsend Bill for a national highway system, but in 1922 it endorsed federal-aid road construction. In 1923 it again voted approval of federal-aid for highways, but in late 1923, it joined with the National Highway Association to distribute a large wall map of the Yellowstone Trail on which is stated: The Yellowstone Trail, a transcontinental highway to be built and forever maintained by the United States government.

In a speech in Sioux Falls, Iowa, in 1926, J.W.Parmley said, "agitation against federal-aid emanates from the eastern states, where mileage is short and revenue long."[2] The West had few people and great distances making it hard to raise even the required matching funds. The clear implication is that the nationwide Association had to work with people of different viewpoints from across the country. Perhaps that explains why the Association's position appears to have vacillated. Road costs were now so high they were completely out of the range of grass roots boosters, so supporting road funding from any and all sources had become a logical policy.

Aids for Tourists

Travel Bureaus

Attracting tourists was the paramount reason to make the Yellowstone Trail successful. Little towns sought tourists to enhance their image of success and growth, to attract settlers, and for economic support. The bigger the tourist numbers, the more highly rated the Trail. To attract a wider audience, the Trail Association opened travel bureaus. In 1917 three had opened, by 1925 there were 15 bureaus in such places as Fort Wayne, Chicago, Milwaukee, Minneapolis, Aberdeen, Miles City, Missoula, and Spokane but only nine bureaus survived by 1928. Travel bureaus were little stations in hotel lobbies or within chambers of commerce. They were manned from May to October by paid assistants who gave away brochures, maps, and road advice. They would even map a trip for people, much like the American Automobile Association does now.

A different version of the travel bureau consisted of tents set up at busy intersections wherein local volunteers performed the same function as the permanent bureau employees.

Yellowstone Trail Association tent travel bureau.
Cover of the 1928 Route Folder

Yet another version was called a "traveling bureau." There were two autos, one traveling east from Minneapolis to Massachusetts, and one west to Seattle. The cars were painted with the Yellowstone Trail logo and colors. They were to be on the move, mostly in camp grounds, rendering assistance and forever encouraging people to take the Yellowstone Trail, leaving a flurry of brochures behind them. They were to help change tires, or with anything a traveler needed, creating good relations for the Trail Association.

The Association also developed a method of keeping track of the number of people using its bureau service while it gave aid to the traveler. Say that a traveling party visiting the Fort Wayne, Indiana travel bureau wished to go to Mobridge, South Dakota. The attendant would supply the party with a current Route Folder containing general information about the Trail Association and a map of the whole Trail, also an area map and a road condition map from Fort Wayne to Chicago. The party would then be advised to visit the Chicago bureau for road conditions and maps to Milwaukee, which office would hand them off to the Minneapolis office, and so on. This way the party would get local road conditions all the way. The party would be encouraged to stop at the small towns in between the travel bureaus, or camp sites, to register themselves. This way the Association could keep apprised of their progress should an emergency arise, and, parenthetically, the Association could keep track of numbers of people served. Numbers were important to success.

In 1917 the three bureaus handled 5,310 inquirers and in 1921 eleven bureaus handled 36,826 inquirers.[3] In 1923, 64,022 inquiries were made of travel bureaus, serving 208,072 individuals with 280,000 expected in 1924.[4] The bureaus figured that they handled only about 40% of the people who actually traveled some distance on the Trail.

The Route Folder was perhaps the most popular item given out at the bureaus. The 50,000 1919 Folders printed were exhausted long before the summer was spent. The Folders contained information about the Trail Association history, mileages between towns, services available in towns, campgrounds, and names of Trailmen in each town. The centerfold map of the entire Trail was most useful, and the insignia reminded the reader of the sign to follow on the highway.

The amount of literature handed out was enormous. During 1923 more than one million pieces were distributed. Included were Folders, United States maps, state maps, road condition maps, and post cards, all printed by the Yellowstone Trail Association to help travelers "see America first."

In 1922 the Trail Association made an arrangement with the Fanum House Information Bureau, Whitcomb Street, London, England to distribute Trail information to people planning a trip to the United States. In return, some travel information about England was available at the Minneapolis office. Similar arrangements were being made in Paris, however, the authors found no further reference to these international ventures.

Trail travel bureaus caught the imagination of many a travel

1919 ROUTE FOLDER 1919

You Don't Need a Log Book to Travel This Road—FOLLOW THE MARKS

The Yellowstone Trail

A Good Road From Plymouth Rock to Puget Sound

| For Auto Business and Tourists | | See America First By This Route |

ONLY AMERICAN HIGHWAY GIVING PERSONAL SERVICE TO TRAVEL.

Free Information Bureaus at
Ft. Wayne, Ind..................Anthony Hotel
Milwaukee, Wis...................Hotel Pfister
Minneapolis, Minn..............Hotel Dyckman
Aberdeen, S. D.............114 So. Lincoln St.
Miles City, Mont..........Chamber of Commerce
Butte, Mont.........................23 Broadway
Missoula, Mont..........Chamber of Commerce
Spokane, Wash..........West 410 Sprague Ave.
AT YOUR SERVICE

THREE NATIONAL PARKS ENROUTE
YELLOWSTONE—GLACIER—MT. RANIER

More improved highway—Better hotels and garages—More beautiful scenery—Better marked—Shorter than any other trans-America highway.
No desert—No stretch without water—Supply towns each twenty miles or nearer—A live representative in each town.
Weekly Road Condition Bulletins
For Information, Address
YELLOWSTONE TRAIL ASSOCIATION, INC.
916 Andrus Building
MINNEAPOLIS, MINNESOTA

FARNHAM PRINTING & STATIONERY CO. MINNEAPOLIS
Republication by John Wm. Ridge. March 2000. Visit www.yellowstonetrail.org

magazine editor. Openings of new bureaus were announced as news items, saving the Association the cost of advertising.

Some interesting characters used the travel bureaus in 1922. Cornelius Vanderbilt followed the Trail from Chicago to Spokane and Walla Walla. Sherman Bond, founder of the Toledo Auto Club, waxed poetic over the "complete services offered by Trail Bureaus" after he traveled from Toledo to Seattle on the Trail. Zane Grey, the novelist, went from Ohio to Seattle registering at several bureaus on the way. A legless chap traveling alone on a motorcycle with a sidecar and camping along the way followed the Trail from Seattle to Syracuse. And then there was the newlywed couple who hiked from Ohio to Montana, planning on taking three months. They were last seen in Miles City, Montana. [5]

Tales of services performed by the bureaus bespeak of personal care unknown today. In South Dakota a tourist lost his spare tires and carrier from the rear of his car 25 miles east of Aberdeen. He reported it to the bureau in Aberdeen. They encouraged the tourist to continue on his way and they would find the tires. The bureau manager advertised in the paper for the lost articles, they were returned, and the touring party was located in Montana. The tires were shipped to Spokane and reunited with their owner. The tourist was amazed.

The retrieval of a pet fox terrier by the Spokane bureau endeared another traveler to the Yellowstone Trail Association, even though he was politely taken to a hardware store for a dog leash.

All the services were performed free. Of course, there were the many stories of people running out of gas at night in the country. "Friendly farmers on the Trail came to the rescue."

Guide Books

Another aid to early autoists was the Automobile Blue Book, published by an independent publishing house, beginning in 1901 and so named because its cover was dark blue. A similar book with a green cover, called, not surprisingly, the Green Book, published by the Scarborough Motor Guide Company, was also available. The Blue Book published three to twelve volumes each year, each covering a section of the United States. A map of known roads in the section was printed in it. The roads were assigned arbitrary "route" numbers. Arranged in a milepost form, the reader selected a "route" and followed the mile-by-mile instructions given. These books performed a valuable service to the traveler because there were very few road maps in the first two decades of the 20th century and no road numbers

Route 935—Erie, Pa., to Cleveland, O.—103.5 m.

Reverse Route 936.

Via Girard, Conneaut, Ashtabula, Geneva, Painesville and Willoughby. Concrete, brick and macadam.

Thru a rolling farming country, following the general shore line of Lake Erie. This is a section of the Yellowstone trail. (Yellow marker with black arrow.)

Miles

0.0 ERIE, State & 6th Sts., at parks. South on State St.

1.4 26th St.; right.

13.1 Fairview. Thru.

17.0 Girard, at monument. Thru.
 GARAGE: F. L. Peters.

22.5 East Springfield, at P. O. Thru.

26.4 West Springfield, Pa., at P. O. Thru.

31.0 Conneaut, O.,* Main & Broad Sts. Thru on Main St.
 GARAGE: City Garage Co.

31.6 Amboy. Thru.

38.9 Kingsville. Thru.

44.0 Left-hand street at far side of park; left.

44.6 Spring St.; right with trolley.

45.1 Ashtabula,* end of street; left onto Main St.
 HOTEL: Warren Hotel.
 GARAGE: Smith's Auto Machine Shop.

45.2 Center St.; right with branch trolley.

45.9 End of street; left.

50.6 Saybrook. Thru.

Miles

55.2 Geneva.* Thru.
 HOTEL: Broadway Inn.
 RESTAURANT: Turner's.
 GARAGE: Geneva Buick Co.

 Caution for RR 56.2.

60.5 North Madison. Thru.

71.4 Right-hand road beyond. RR underpass; right.

72.9 Painesville,* irreg. 4-cor at small green. Right with trolley.
 HOTEL: Parmly.
 GARAGE: W. M. Voegtler Motor Sales.
 Sharp left at 72.9 leads to business center.

79.6 Mentor, at courthouse. Thru.
 HOTEL: Broadlawn Inn.

83.4 Willoughby, Vine & Erie Sts. Thru on Vine St.

86.8 End of road; left onto Lake Shore Blvd.

93.5 4-cor.; right.

94.7 4-cor.; right with trolley.

95.3 5-cor., trolley leaves to left; thru onto main drive thru park.

These towns with Points of Interest are arranged alphabetically, pages 500-564.

A typical page of an Automobile Blue Book. This is from page 783 of Vol. 1, 1922. This route is identified as being part of the Yellowstone Trail.

at all until 1918 when Wisconsin set a precedent for the United States. Instructions relied upon sites along the road as well as named trails. There had to be another person in the car to call out the instructions to the driver. Unfortunately, "turn left at the red school" does not help the modern traveler to follow the Trail.

The Yellowstone Trail Association arranged with the Blue Book publishers to log the entire Trail from Chicago to Seattle. The Association agreed to provide the transportation and driver to carry the Blue Book representative at such speed as he would dictate. Thus it was that in June 1915 a Blue Book mapper found himself speeding down Sheridan Road on the Chicago-Seattle relay speed run described in Chapter Two. They joined the race in Chicago, but at the city limits dropped back to conduct their mapping and describing job, going west for the next two months. Apparently the Blue Book representative made progress because the *Ismay* [Montana] *Journal* of July 30, 1915 spoke of a Mr. Woodall who had been escorted around the Mildred-Fallon-Terry area. He assured all that the Yellowstone Trail would be given "due recognition in the next issue of the Blue Book."[6] And so the Trail was first included in the Blue Book in 1916 and would remain in subsequent Blue Books until 1929.

At first the books were thick, explaining every mile and turn and landmark. One 1919 Blue Book, for instance, ran 1284 pages, including area and city maps and short city descriptions. As numbered and marked roads came into existence, the user needed only to read, "follow US 137 to state 16." Thus, by 1929 the Blue Book was very thin, 130 pages including advertisements, maps, and area descriptions. It was in the process of being replaced by the oil company folded map.

Maps

The first printed American map specifically showing automobile routes appeared in the *Chicago Times-Herald* in 1895 to show the course of a local auto race.[7] In the 1890's the bicycling craze caused the League of American Wheelmen to produce road maps, designed to keep cyclists out of the mud, for areas around some cities. Since early autos were mainly driven in cities, there was little thought of long distance travel and little need for road maps. State and national maps featured railroad routes only.

By the early 1920's, road maps were becoming relatively common. The oil companies had found that free maps for tourists were an essential marketing tool. Free maps were common until the 1970's. Cartographic companies, primary among which was the Rand McNally company, found huge markets. They produced the oil company maps, maps for a wide range of companies needing to advertise, and maps for sale to individuals.

The Yellowstone Trail Association laid out the Trail in minute detail from Minneapolis to Bozeman, Montana and published the mapped results in their *First Year Book of the Twin Cities-Aberdeen-Yellowstone Park Trail 1914*. The Automobile Club of Southern California published equally detailed strip maps following the Yellowstone Trail from Minneapolis to the Yellowstone Park in 1920. The Automobile Club of Western Washington published strip maps of the Trail from Spokane to the Yellowstone Park in 1922. These maps featured mileages between sites and blowups of town maps, along with a few scenic and man-made attractions noted along the route.

In 1922 the Association published 18 different maps, including maps of states adjacent to the Trail showing their connecting routes, the map of the entire Trail in the popular annual Folder, and road condition maps. They also published "touring maps" for the states along the Trail.

THE YELLOWSTONE TRAIL
TOURING SERVICE
Map No. 9   ———   Minnesota

FIGURES BETWEEN TOWNS INDICATE MILEAGE

Stick to the Yellowstone Trail -- When it is bad we will tell you

ALL YELLOWSTONE TRAIL PUBLICATIONS ARE FREE

Published by THE YELLOWSTONE TRAIL ASSOCIATION   ·   ·   ·   ·   337-339 Andrus Building, Minneapolis

Large wall maps of the whole interstate Trail, 3 feet tall by 4 feet wide, were produced in conjunction with the National Highway Association. They were designed for hotels, garages, chambers of commerce, and Trail bureaus. They contained mileages between larger cities along the whole of the Trail from Plymouth Rock to Puget Sound.

Another map the Trail Association circulated regularly to hotels, garages, and to others was the "road condition map." This large map showed the whole Trail with cities noted on the map only if an advertising contract was purchased by some organization in that city. The map was partitioned

Yellowstone Trail Association Road Condition Map Service

H. O. COOLEY, General Agent   CORRECTED EACH WEEK   By the Yellowstone Trail Association, Aberdeen, So. Dak.

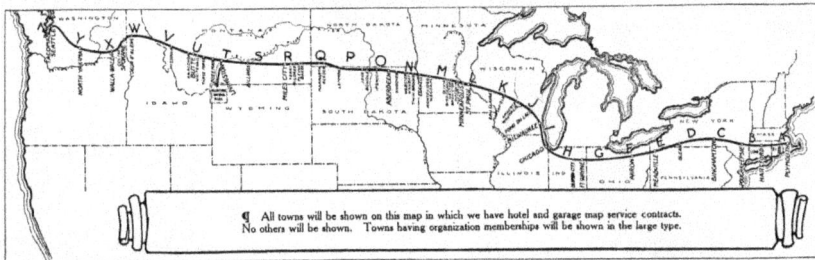

¶ All towns will be shown on this map in which we have hotel and garage map service contracts. No others will be shown. Towns having organization memberships will be shown in the large type.

Hotels and Garages
ENROUTE
AT WHICH THIS SERVICE WILL BE FOUND.
Towns from East to West.

¶ This space will be taken up by the names of towns, and hotels and garages in those towns, with which we have map service contracts.

Map Division
JUL 1 1918
Library of Congress

Key to Road Conditions
1—Good Improved.
2—Good Natural.
3—Heavy.
4—Rain or Snow.
5—Washout, inquire at
6—Construction Work, inquire at
7—Poorly Marked.
8—Inquire Each Town.

¶ This space for pasting gummed topped weekly report.

THE HOTELS AND GARAGES ABOVE HAVE MADE THIS SERVICE POSSIBLE, AND DESERVE YOUR PATRONAGE.

into about 125 mile segments labeled A, B, C, etc. There were eight codes of condition on the map: 1=good improved, 2=good natural, 3=heavy (muddy), 4=rain or snow, 5=washout, 6=construction work, 7=poorly marked, 8=inquire in each town. A changeable portion, which the garage owner pasted to the lower right corner of the map, noted weekly road condition changes. A driver in Ohio could therefore check on road conditions in, say, Billings, Montana.

Each garage or hotel or company along the Trail that paid for a map was given advertising space. A free map was also sent to one non-profit organization such as the chamber of commerce or city campground or automobile club for each advertising contract completed for that town. In 1922 about 600 maps, 300 paid for and 300 free, were prepared. This map making arrangement publicized the Trail in the practical way that it paid for itself. The weekly updates were prepared at headquarters by means of telegraphed data from local Trailmen. Each map recipient received a weekly update which, in 1922, created 31,200 pieces of mail plus telegrams generated for just this one of the Association's many projects. The Association produced these maps for about 10 years and claimed to be the only trail association doing so.

Yellowstone Campground in Stevens Point, Wisconsin
Photo from private collection.

Auto Camping

An unknown writer in *Outing Magazine* in 1924, said that "The automobile has revolutionized the average American's vacation, it has brought about a renaissance of the outdoors, and it has firmly planted a brand-new sport." The highway led to the great outdoors and the brand-new sport was auto camping.

Warren Belasco, social commentator, has written extensively on the history of auto camping, reminding the reader that early camping was called "gypsying," "motor hoboing" and "vagabonding."[8] Mostly, the recreational auto camper of 1910-1920 was of the middle class who could afford to stay in hotels but who chose to cast off the strictures of schedules, dressing for dinner and forced sociability. They were, as Belasco said, "Thoreau at 29 cents a gallon."[9] "Vagabonding" tales of daring and carefree abandon were breathtakingly told in such magazines as *Outing, American Motorist, Western Tourist* and in the camper's hometown newspaper, further spreading the allure of camping.

Even travel over the poorest roads sounded enticing. William Bettis described such a 1922 road in Wisconsin as he traveled from Toledo to Seattle on the Yellowstone Trail. The road through Menomonie to Wilson, on his way to Hudson, was "ground to a fine powder, owing to lack of rain, that in places was six to eight inches deep. There were many cars coming and going, and everyone was doing its [sic] best to scatter the road over the adjacent fields. The air was filled with dust." Bettis also advised campers to arrive in daylight as, at Hudson, they got on the wrong road to the camp which lead him winding up a high hill in the dark to a spot marked NO CAMPING. They camped anyway.[10]

Journalist Frank Wentworth took three years off to tour the nation by camping. From 1924-1927 he roamed leisurely in his "Tin Lizzie" and "Tin Lizzie II" describing in minute detail his trip, road conditions, and each campground and its denizens. His was not an alluring tale, but realistic, funny and romantic in its tales of courage and creativity in overcoming adversity.[11]

In the early days of auto travel, some camped by the roadside wherever they happened to be at sundown, leaving fouled streams and a mess of tin cans for the farmer to clean up. Some campers broke off fruit tree branches, stole fruits and vegetables, flowers, and anything else not tied down. Camping guides, in 1923, began to include words about "camping ethics" and a farmer posted this message: "Notis. Trespassers will B persecuted to the full extent of 2 mongrel dogs which never was over sochible to strangers and 1 doubl brl shot gun which ain't loaded with sofa pillors. Dam if I ain't gotten tired of this hell raisin on my place."[12]

The usual scenario of communities providing campgrounds ran something like this: a local commercial club or chamber of commerce would realize that most campers were founts of money so their presence in the community was treasured. A campground was the vehicle to allow them to share in the spoils of this new anti-establishment sport. To get campers off the roadside where they were unmindful of private land, city fathers found land for a free campground, usually as part of the city park, which was downtown and close to merchants. Volunteers manned them. In a very short time, campers demanded more services such as running water, hot plates, kitchens, covered picnic areas, showers, etc. It is estimated that there were 3,000-6,000 municipal auto camps in business during 1920-1924.[13] As numbers of campers climbed and were proudly printed in the weekly newspaper, communities began charging for the services they installed and hired a caretaker "to keep the rif-raf out."

The Yellowstone Trail Association had been encouraging the towns along the Trail to host free city-managed campgrounds. By 1921 the Association was quietly encouraging the same towns to charge small fees, and the Trailman was asked to inspect the camp to ensure that the good name of the Trail remained intact.

Some small towns could not keep up with demands and closed down their campgrounds. Around 1924 some put time limits on sites when undesirables arrived and actually moved into the free camp, not leaving. Private entrepreneurs began establishing campgrounds in a more rural setting, adding cabins to the amenities and adding competition to city-run sites. By 1922 there were 600 tourist auto courts,[14] and the motel was born. In the 1930's some cabins sported coverings between them to house autos. For those still seeking solitude in the wilds, some national parks and national forests provided campgrounds as the federal government built more roads into the interior of its lands. Yellowstone Park and Yosemite and others were also providing "permanent camps" with wood floors, heat, a restaurant, and maid service.

According to a 1924 article in *The Arrow*, a monthly newsletter publication by the Yellowstone Trail Association, tourism was becoming a major business. Minnesota reported that in 1923, 300,000 tourists left about $16 million in the state. Spokane and Seattle reported 97,000 campers left about $5-$7 per day per person.[15]

Camping outfits ran the gamut from simply strapping suitcases to the running board to fancy, fully outfitted cars running into the hundreds of dollars for proper clothing and equipment. *Motor Age* of April 5, 1917 printed a ten-page spread about all the camping equipment needed. The AAA *Official Camping Manual* of 1922 offered 85 pages of camping advice about equipment, behavior, health, maps, national parks, and camp sites along the major named trails and highways.

A surprising item recommended in 1917 was the trailer. Trailers ranged from something that looked like a small U-Haul to, in 1922, a sumptuous home on wheels. This motor home was built by the owner, as were most trailers until the middle 1930's. It weighed 9,000 pounds and featured all the comforts of home such as screens, a bath, and heat in its 6x6x8 feet. It had a maximum speed of 40mph and got 12 miles to the gallon. It also got headlines wherever it went, especially on the Yellowstone Trail.[16]

Just as the advent of the auto itself was a great democratizer, so, too, was the popularity of camping, numbering an estimated five

Camping in the Bitterroots
Courtesy of the Mineral County Historical Society

million in 1922. The poor used camping as a cheap way to travel. The middle class chose camping as a great getaway, an unusual experience. The growing number of wealthy campers may have brought creature comforts with them in the way of chauffeurs and staff, but they were out under the same stars as their poorer neighbors. *The American Motorist* of September 1920 made a direct appeal to the wealthy Easterner to forsake the usual summer tour of crowded hotels and resorts and go camping. Other magazines made an open pitch to women, assuring them of family safety and easy kitchen work.

It is not surprising that health problems arose early on. At first, there were no privies and people just used fields or the roadside as a toilet. By the mid-1920's a serious auto camping health crisis was in evidence. In Yellowstone Trail states of Indiana and Minnesota things were not good. The Indiana State Board of Health ruled that 27% of the 116 camp grounds visited had water unfit to drink and more than 50% had inadequate sewage and garbage disposal systems.[17] In "Tourist Camps and Public Health" in *Western Magazine* of November 1922, a "problem of epic proportion" was reported. In addition to the problem of poor water and waste disposal, Minnesota was worried about strangers bringing in disease, citing a precipitous rise in typhoid fever cases over earlier years when camping was not as popular.

An exultant song of praise to the sport of camping was sung by botanist Clarence Wedge in his article, "Camping on the Yellowstone Trail" in *The Minnesota Horticulturalist* of October 1916. For 25 years he and his family had spent his month's vacation camping in the upper Midwest and West chronicling the flora and enjoying the absence of people and creature comforts. This first trip on the Yellowstone Trail led him to conclude that "one of the principle charms about the great country traversed by the Yellowstone Trail is its newness and freshness. Millions of acres just as the Indian, the buffalo and the coyote left them - broad stretches as far as eye can reach without a sign of human habitation. But this is fast passing away." [18]

Safety on the Yellowstone Trail

Any way one looked at it, safety was a problem for early autoists. The combination of fragile cars, inexperienced drivers, speeds up to 60 mph, railroad crossings and bad roads became lethal. Thousands of deaths each year became a matter of national discussion and half-hearted actions.

Railroad crossings posed the greatest danger. There was hardly a day that newspapers did not report an often-fatal collision. Crossings were unmarked while railroad companies and counties argued over whose responsibility it was to mark them. When trains became express, speeding through little villages where once they stopped, the speed prevented a safe stopping distance. The most common cause of accidents was driver error, of young men succumbing to testosterone and trying to "beat the train." Leslie Childs, legal editor for the *American Motorist Magazine,* averred that the courts had placed the responsibility upon the motorist unless the driver can show he is free of contributory negligence.[19]

Poor judgment rode shotgun with many drivers on the Trail. In a small area of rural North Dakota in 1925, 30 accidents involving autos and trains were recorded, 14 wherein autos crashed into trains, some of which were standing still, and 16 wherein trains crashed into autos in spite of functioning flagmen, barriers and bells. All were caused by driver error. In one case a driver drove around a stopped truck, drove through the barrier, ignored the flagman, and drove into the moving train. Flagmen were authorized to arrest such drivers. A reporter observed, "It is strange that it should be necessary to arrest auto drivers in order to get them to protect their own lives."[20]

"Turning turtle" was another accident of the times along the Trail. Flipping a car over was apparently easy to do, given a combination of a high center of gravity on the auto, a road with too high a crown, deep drainage ditches, and an inexperienced driver. Again, speed seems to have been the culprit in most cases. With little protection for the occupants, not even side windows or a roof in the early days, fatalities mounted.

The road itself could cause hair-raising experiences. Most roads were only 16 feet wide and flanked by deep ditches, allowing vehicles to pass only at very slow speeds. Grades and banks on curves provided, for an out-of-control car, a ride up the bank and off the road. Human error, again, caused the death of a young man who was standing on the left running board while his friend sped along a curvy, forest road. At one right-hand turn, the car skidded and slammed the rider into a tree. And then there was the story of a young couple who had attended a dance and fell asleep on the way home. The car settled into ruts on the muddy road and idled along on its own, the car turning where the ruts took it until the closed barn door loomed up in front of them in the dark.

The first centerline on a rural state highway was painted between Marquette and Ishpeming, Michigan in 1917,[21] but the idea was not immediately endorsed. They really were needed. In a 1928 news item in a Hector, Minnesota, paper the public was advised in a headline to "Keep to the Right on Pavement." Many drivers just straddled the crowned center or were confused, which lead to any number of accidents. One woman driver could not decide which side of the road to select, so chose the zig-zag route, causing two accidents, one in front of her and one behind.

Another accident in a Trail town was reported to have been caused by a driver turning a corner and heading down the left lane "and then at times turned partly to head into the right lane, confusing Mr. Bremmer who was in that lane. Both drivers became excited and turned toward each other, resulting in a head-on collision.[22] An accident in 1925 was caused because two cars did not have headlights and were driving on a dark night. Speeds were such that the cars were "interlocked" and several passengers were thrown 50 feet. Front seat riders were shoved under dashboards in both cars.[23]

In the 1920's, fatal accidents kept pace with the growth of the auto industry, reaching 20,000 deaths by 1924. Many windshields had no wipers and needed to be opened by hand to see in inclement weather, which distracted drivers. Brake bands failed frequently; tires lead shorter lives than fruit flies. And then there was the crank used to start the engine. If you lost your grip, a broken arm was often the result. If you had your thumb on one side and your fingers on the other, that thumb might have a short life. No wonder women did not take much to driving until the electric starter was invented.

Uniform traffic rules were proven necessary early on. Traffic rules of twenty-five large cities were studied. Speed limits in cities varied from eight to 25 mph. In 11 cities, one blast of a traffic cop's whistle allowed east-west traffic to proceed while in 14 cities, the same signal allowed north-south traffic to proceed. Headlight usage and passing rules also varied widely.[24] Road magazines in the late 1920's featured many articles clucking about safety problems, but no broad-scaled solutions appeared.

Long, slow improvement in auto safety and convenience was dawning, though. Axles were less likely to break. Safety glass didn't shatter into vicious slivers. Hydraulic brakes were reasonably effective. In 1923 windshield wipers allowed one to drive without sticking one's head outside. Tie rods stayed connected—usually. However, protruding knobs and steering columns which impaled drivers were to last longer. And seat belts were decades away. Road safety conditions were at least talked about. Bridge abutments should not be right at the edge of the pavement. Right angle turns at rural section line intersections should be curved. The width of the road should allow two vehicles to safely pass. Centerlines, curves, corners and road problems should be marked.

These had, indeed, been "grand years." Prohibition and the "roaring '20's" co-existed. Nationally, women could vote. Charlie Chaplin was riding high and talking motion pictures were on the horizon. The eight-hour workday was coming in and Jack Dempsey was champ. The 1921 Federal-Aid Highway Act ensured a future for road funding. But the "grand years" ended with a threat to trail organizations. A threat that was to end the lives of many such organizations and change the character of others, such as the Yellowstone Trail Association. US road numbers were arriving.

Endnotes

1. Department of Transportation, America's Highways: 1776-1976. A History of the Federal-Aid Program (Washington, DC: U.S. Govt. Printing Office 1976) 206.

2. J.W. Parmley speech before the State Telephone Association, Sioux Falls, January 13, 1926.

3. Western Magazine Vol 18 1921: 135.

4. R.B. Anderson, Director of Bureaus, manuscript for Outer's Recreational Magazine, Spring 1924. (South Dakota State Historical Society. Parmley Papers SC10, Folder #2 , entitled Yellowstone Trail Association 1914-1939).

5. Western Magazine 18 (1922).

6. Ismay Journal July 30, 1915:-1 reprint from Fallon Forum.

7. Walter W. Ristow, "American Maps and Road Guides" The Scientific Monthly 62 (1946) 397 as quoted in James R. Ackerman monograph "Selling Maps, Selling Highways: Rand McNally's 'Blazed Trails' Program," Imago Mundi 45 (1993) 81.

8. Warren James Belasco (1979) Americans on the Road: From Autocamp to Motel 1910-1945. (Cambridge, Massachusetts: MIT Press. 1979) 7.

9. Ibid.

10. William C. Bettis. A Trip to the Pacific Coast by Automobile, Camping on the Way. (Toledo: Booth Typesetting Co. 1922) 13.

11. Frank L. Wentworth. On the Road With Lizzie (Iowa City, Iowa: Mercer Printing Co., 1930).

12. Belasco 75.

13. Allan D. Wallis Wheel Estate: The Rise and Decline of Mobile Homes. (New York: Oxford Univ. Press, 1991) 39.

14. Poyntz Tyler, ed. American Highways Today The Reference Shelf 29:1. (New York: The H.W. Wilson Co.,1957) 39.

15. Frank E. Brimmer, "The Value of the Yellowstone Trail to the Traveling Public of America," The Arrow May, 1924.

16. Mineral Independent Aug. 10, 1922.

17. Belasco 118.

18. Clarence Wedge, "Camping on the Yellowstone Trail," The Minnesota Horticulturalist 44:10 (Oct. 1916):361-366.

19. Leslie Childs quoted in Western Magazine XII:6 Dec.1, 1918.

20. Marmarth Mail October 2, 1925:2.

21. America's Highways 127.

22. Colby [Wisconsin] Phonograph, April 24, 1919:1.

23. Marmarth Mail October 9, 1925:1.

24. Motor Age April 12, 1917:26.

Chapter Five

1926 - 1930   The End of the Trail

The Yellowstone Trail had been an idea born out of a necessity that was ending. One death knell of all trail organizations was the advent of government numbered routes. Another was, only partially, the Great Depression. Governmental structures were now in place to facilitate and organize road building, funding, route marking and mapping. Commercial travel agencies and a vastly grown AAA performed travel services for the whole country. Other matters were now occupying the minds of Trail boosters.

The Effect of Governmental Numbering of Highways

With numbers replacing names for long distance routes, feelings of trail ownership, allegiance, and camaraderie faded. The romance and adventure of auto travel to distant places were being replaced by an acceptance of auto travel as the new necessity for practical living.

Excessive trail marking had made the system dysfunctional. Duplication of road marking resulted from the activities of over 250 trail organizations. One road might bear the colored symbols of several trail organizations. For example, 70% of one trail overlapped other marked routes and one trail overlapped 11 others. One road carried eight different trail markers.[1] Some trails had alternate routes, adding confusion to their own marking system. The Yellowstone Trail Association, however, had rejected the confusion of alternate routes early on. However, in 1915, so many trails had claimed the northern corridor skirting Lake Erie that the Yellowstone Trail was refused admittance. In spite of several trails on one route, the traveler often lacked consistent highway information.

Such chaos in marking! Pressures were being placed on state highway commissions by trail organizations to support "their" road. This resulted, in 1925, in the Department of Agriculture's Bureau of Public Roads and the American Association of State Highway Officials (AASHO) joining to formulate a numbering and marking system for principal interstate roads. This created the national highway system, with the US shield on its markers that we see today.

This Joint Board sought information from the states to identify roads within their borders that could be interstate and of national significance. The Board then settled on the now-familiar pattern of numbering east-west roads with even numbers beginning from the north. Thus, US 2 runs near the Canadian border; US 98 skirts the Gulf of Mexico. North-south roads were given odd numbers from east to west. Thus, US 1 hugs the east coast and US 101 the west coast. However, there are many exceptions. The Joint Board's plan was accepted by states, after emendations, bringing the system of marked roads up to 96,626 miles. On November 11, 1926, the plan was approved by the Joint Board and immediately put into effect. It was a cooperative state-federal numbering system of state highways, devised mainly by state engineers, not a federal government system as widely believed, although the signs bore the US shield.

Numbers on highways had not been unknown. Wisconsin had been numbering and marking its roads since 1918, the first state to do so. The majority of states had followed Wisconsin's system, each working within its boundaries with occasional synchronization of major routes with neighboring states. Washington State had numbered its roads for the convenience of the highway department engineers, but did not post those numbers for travelers to use.

The trail organizations fought to have a single number applied to their trails, hoping to retain the name along with the new number. This was not to be and the Yellowstone Trail succumbed to a great variety of numbers, with US 12 assigned to the Trail in South Dakota, part of Montana and a bit of Wisconsin. To this day some people believe that US 12 constitutes the whole of the old Trail, simply because it was so numbered in their area. In truth, under the initial 1926 plan, the Yellowstone Trail was given nine US numbers and a great variety of state and county numbers.

The End of the Trail

The usefulness of trail organizations faded and disappeared as their missions were replaced by governmental and professional travel agencies. At the time of its formation, the Yellowstone Trail Association had four main purposes for existing: to cause its long-distance route to be constructed across the nation, to see that road-building was funded by government money, to attract tourists to the Yellowstone Trail, and to see a web of roads encompassing the whole nation. The Association saw these things accomplished. A useable, practical route from Plymouth Rock to Puget Sound was developed. Road financing had been assumed by various levels of government. Tourists were being drawn to the Trail. A web of connected routes existed to almost every corner of the country.

It is readily obvious that no one can legitimately claim that the Yellowstone Trail Association was singularly responsible for the successful conclusion of all four goals, but it did play its role admirably in translating grass roots needs and opinions into national policy. Parmley and his associates were the right people in the right place at the right time.

There is every sign that the founders and leaders of the Association enjoyed their long effort. They were both good at it and believers in the cause. Their Association was undoubtedly strengthened by continuing adversity, primary among which was lack of finances. The group had been plagued with financial problems its whole life. The year 1921 was a period of national recession and the Trail Association survived. But in the late 1920's, that same problem served as another death knell. As early as January 1926, almost a year before the Joint Board of AASHO and Bureau of Public Roads engineers replaced names with numbers, a desperate bulletin was issued by General Manager H.O. Cooley to the membership at large. In it he stated that he would feature one town each week in the bulletin that was in arrears in paying its assessment. He called it the Debt Paying Bulletin and likened paying debts unto a game in which he was the scorekeeper and would publish names of debtors for the featured town of the week. He proceeded to do so, in which process he probably embarrassed and alienated more than he shamed into paying up. In August of 1927 a financial report showed that almost $16,000 had been collected and spent in eight months, leaving a debt of $1338 in spite of a membership of 7789. The report also showed a cancellation of membership by 155 people. At the end of 1929, the financial report showed receipts and expenditures of about $11,500. The good news was that they were out of debt with a balance of $11.99 to carry forward. The previous year they had had a balance of $18 to carry forward. The organization never expected to see a profit, but the annual fight for solvency must have been wearing.

In late 1927 and early 1928 there was a spate of letters between W.J. Mulvaney, then president of the Association, and J.W. Parmley, founder, third president and senior consultant on any matter pertaining to the Trail Association. The letters revealed the sad news that Parmley was, apparently, being denied a look at the books, denied any information about a promised audit, and was receiving no answers to his letters to General Manager

Cooley. Parmley suspected that Cooley never ordered an outside audit, perhaps due to lack of the necessary $300. His disappointment, bitterness, and anger spilled over, causing Mulvaney to respond with patient advice that running a national organization should raise a man above personal pejoratives. Parmley's requests never seemed to have been honored by either Mulvaney or Cooley.

Mulvaney, in a March 7, 1928 letter to Parmley, wonders if there is a future for the Trail organization:

> Personally, I am undecided whether it is going to be worthwhile to keep the Yellowstone Trail going or not. If it does keep going, it is going to take some real effort on the part of every part of the country through which it travels. . . . if the Yellowstone Trail ever needed friends it needs them now if it is to continue. So it looks like it is going to be up to the people along the trail whether to continue to exist or not. . . . if we don't all pull together it is sure to pass out of the picture. [2]

Parmley answered that there is a lack of confidence on the part of the membership in the people who are running the organization, people who do not appeal to the former ardent supporters.

Parmley had a hard time understanding what was happening to the organization that he worked night and day to promote, putting his own money into it at every turn, guiding its decisions to create this great route. What was causing the organization to grind to a halt? Was it lack of proper funding? Was it shaken confidence in present leadership? Was it the new national road numbering system that took the steam out of private road groups all over the nation?

The camaraderie and sense of "doing it ourselves" were slipping from their hands. There was no pride of accomplishment, no allegiance for a mere highway number. There was no collegial history of a US 10. There was no need for yellow paint and local painters anymore. County government could no longer be influenced by a Marcus Beebe plunking down $500 for his road. Efficiency of route was replacing Main Street boosters - an efficiency that was beginning to bypass Main Street altogether.

In spite of financial woes and personal feuds, General Manager Cooley persevered, speaking in Aberdeen, South Dakota in December of 1929, in his usual role as chief cheerleader. He reported surprisingly good news for an organization on its last legs. He listed all of the western states hosting the Trail and reported upwards of 85% assessments paid, with Idaho coming in at 109%. And 95% of Montana's roads were federal, graveled, and much of them oiled.[3] He did not sound like a man who would resign three and a half months later, nor did he reveal to his audience the gravity of his worries.

The Yellowstone Trail Association had been incorporated January 26, 1918 with eleven Directors of the Corporation named. However, it seems that the Directors did not function as directors: they never met as directors, they never had elections for successors, they never ordered audits and never signed off on tax reports, apparently. Their function seemed to have been replaced, in part, by the Executive Committee which membership was elected annually from state meetings, and which guided the membership. As a result, Cooley, as the only constant and salaried employee, was left alone to manage the funds, all of the advertising, and to administer publicity bureaus of this national organization. For years Cooley's name had been synonymous with the Trail. He visited every state, Executive Committee and annual meeting; he appeared as a very entertaining and informed guest speaker at every town on the Trail. He was indefatigable, devoted, honest and interesting as he juggled his many hats. If the organization was having trouble, it should have been up to the long-forgotten Directors of the Corporation and not the General Manager to call for an audit, or to dissolve the organization.

Information about the organization became very scarce after 1925. Their famous Route Folder was printed in 1925, but the authors can find no copies nor references to copies between that year and 1928. Officers listed in the 1928 Folder were the same as in the 1925 Folder, leading us to think that there were no elections held between '25 and '28. The Executive Committee business was carried on by mail in 1927 and the state chapters were asked to discuss and forward their opinions upon the topic: Shall the Yellowstone Trail Association liquidate its business and cease to exist, or shall work plans for 1928 be adopted? The answer from the states apparently was "proceed on work plans" because an Executive Committee still existed in 1928 and the organization did not dissolve for another two and a half years.

There were no records of a 1929 annual meeting found by the authors. With no viable organization left, Cooley was left alone, again, this time to close the office of the organization. And he did so on March 15, 1930.

In his letter of resignation, addressed, for reasons that are now unclear, to a Mr. Dahlman of Lemmon, South Dakota, he pointed out that none of the states had scheduled meetings that year, and there was no plan for an annual meeting. There was no income, and, in fact, the organization was $6176.45 in debt. He had to leave the office furniture in lieu of office rent, but did take away a typewriter, a few pictures and the trademark that was copyrighted in his name. A truckload of office records was delivered to

Parmley and he offered their examination to anyone. Unfortunately, only a very slim file remains of those records in the South Dakota State Historical Society Library.

It was not the advent of the Depression *per se* that created the grim financial future for the group. In fact, small town newspapers all along the Trail made no note of October's Black Thursday nor of people throwing themselves off of high buildings. In mid-September, an Associated Press item warning about the rapid growth in the number of combines or mergers and consolidations appeared in the *Marmarth Mail*, [4] but other newspapers were silent about the happenings of faraway Wall Street until the local banks began closing and local stock prices fell some months later. It was not the Depression alone that caused the Trail's demise. But probably it would have been the ultimate cause had the Trail Association not closed its doors before the brunt of the storm arrived.

It must have stung Cooley immeasurably to learn that Aberdeen, the stalwart supporter and early home of the Yellowstone Trail Association headquarters, pulled out of the organization in January of 1930.

In July 1930, four months after Cooley resigned, Parmley wrote letters to the editors of the newspapers along the Trail, wherein he briefly related his version of the demise of the Trail organization. The venom was there, couched in sadness. He blamed bad management (actually the management by Cooley) and a lack of resolve by the membership who mistakenly believed that there was no more to be done now that the federal government was pitching in. But, more important, he hinted that a new Yellowstone Trail organization may be in the making, unrelated to the old, unrelated to the mistakes of the old. His letter asked his old friends along the Trail what they thought of another try at it. He harkened back to the old, linking it to the new:

> Would we have had the road today had men not got behind it and urged its building? The fact is that it is paved or graveled from the Atlantic to McLaughlin, South Dakota. Would this have been the case without concerted effort? There is, I believe, as much work to be done as at its inception. Paving is coming. The gaps west must be closed. Ditches must be filled. Officials must be urged to care for the public needs. Maps must be furnished to the public, marking renewed through an organization extending down from mile 3800 to the last mile. [5]

The fire was back in the belly. In 1930, at 69 years of age, Parmley was about to embark upon a new highway booster campaign. Oddly, Parmley was not the only one who thought that there was a role left for trail organizations, even though the trails were now nameless national numbers. As late as 1935 a writer cited several reasons for the existence of trail organizations. Multiplicity of numbers along a single route was his first point. There were more than 30 different state and US highway numbers on the Yellowstone Trail between Plymouth Rock and Puget Sound. So the trail markings still served a purpose; "If you see the black arrow on yellow you know you are on the right road." [6]

Other trail supporters thought that the truth about road conditions could be published by trail organizations, as the Yellowstone Trail Association had done for years. Free maps are always welcome to the traveler. National highways still needed local advocates to check on conditions, travelers still needed to know about the natural attractions along certain routes, highway beautification programs could exist. Communities still could benefit from tourist visits. The Trail Association had accomplished so much in the past, that influence still could be used, albeit through the creation of a new organization.

The Yellowstone Highway Association

The Articles of Incorporation for this new organization were filed by Joe Parmley on September 5, 1930 containing the purpose for which the corporation was formed. Briefly, the purpose was to: promote the interests of the Yellowstone Trail; aid in its improvement, change, or abandonment; cooperate with government to get it paved; eliminate places of danger; map it; preserve historic places along the Trail; and promote tourism.[7] It was to be a public benefit corporation with no capital stock and no public liability; money would only be pledged for its promotional work. [8]

Directors were former members of the old organization. Correspondence revealed that Parmley called upon old Trail acquaintances for help with the new effort. He saw no reason to change the *modus operandi* of the past organization. Nor was the name of the road changed. Having spent 18 years building the name of the Yellowstone Trail in the hearts and minds of the traveling public, he found no reason to change it to Yellowstone Highway. In some cases, the press called the road Yellowstone Trail, Highway 12 or Yellowstone Trail, Highway 10. One confused headline writer called it the Yellowstone Highway Trail. For years after the Yellowstone *Highway* Association was created, newspapers mistakenly called it the Yellowstone *Trail* Association. News articles in 1935 dealing with paving US 12 still reminded the reader that the road was the Yellowstone Trail.

The new organization's first and constant task was to harry local, state and federal highway officials to close the gaps in the hard surface of the Yellowstone Trail, of which there were many, and at least to oil the hundreds of miles of gravel. In a 1934 letter to the South Dakota Emergency Relief and Civil Works Administration Committee, Parmley requested a copy of the law which gave South Dakota $6 million for roads out of $400 million appropriated by Congress. He was probably searching for support for hard surfacing his road. He was told to write to Washington for the law.

The new organization also continued marking the road with yellow paint. Twenty-eight gallons were shipped to Miles City in November of 1930 for distribution.[9]   In 1932, Northern Power and Light Company of Mobridge gave them permission to paint a 15 inch Yellowstone Trail logo on their poles but prohibited metal signs.[10] Mounting a publicity campaign, again, was also on their plate. The new publicity man was assigned the task of writing articles for travel, outdoor, and auto magazines, in addition to newspapers along the Trail. Mailings to the membership took the form of newsletters entitled "The Yellowstone Trail." Public meetings were held to promote enthusiasm. And, of course, there was the call for membership dues, their new pledge slips looking very familiar. Even the Yellowstone Trail logo was retained, in spite of the fact that H.O. Cooley claimed to own it personally. The approach was the same, but the problem had changed. Can David's weapon slay this new Goliath?

The 1935 Folder, reminiscent of the popular Route Folder given to tourists a decade before, was the last Folder published that the authors have been able to find. In 1937 the leadership was, essentially, the same as that of 1930. Newspapers were no longer interested in the organization that brought their little towns out of the mud and brought them tourists and a bit of fame. Newspapers of the1930's along the old western Trail were interested in their local, numbered *road* and costs to repair it; they were not interested in a national *route*. Oil company maps gave them routes now.

The Yellowstone Highway Association was up against more formidable odds than its predecessor organization ever had to face. All of the advertising, meetings, news coverage, and boosterism in the world could not have overcome the effects of the Great Depression and the Dust Bowl of the '30s. All of the grief and misery of a proud nation come to ground made mere survival paramount. The following 1933 letter from a loyal Trail member from the Star Garage of Missoula, Montana at once reflected and foretold the times:

I was a member of the Yellowstone Trail Association for a number of years and a booster for the same, but times have changed since that was the only marked trail across this state. Now the highways are numbered and there is not the interest in the Yellowstone Trail. Some goof even painted out a lot of the Trail markings in this section before he could be stopped.

I am not financially able to give any assistance in this enterprise at the present time and that is the principal [sic] boosting that you need. I can and will give out maps and shall be pleased to help in paying for them at a later date if that will be any help to you, but I cannot say to what extent, for business is very light and I do not know how soon it will revive.

That the organization stumbled along until 1937 is amazing in itself.

US 12 Association

An April 29, 1937 meeting postponed the arrival of the knacker man and proved that the Trail body was not quite dead. That day highway officials from three states along the Trail met to discuss the needs of US Highway 12 regarding oiling and paving. These were the very topics the Yellowstone Highway Association had been pushing with, at best, marginal success for the previous seven years. Present also were members of state and county civic organizations and county boards. Joe Parmley was invited and before the day was out he was asked to organize a group to press governmental agencies regarding the needs of US Highway 12 in Minnesota and the Dakotas.

At age 76 he was off and running - again! Parmley was made president, a set of officers and directors was appointed and 33 representatives from the three states were on board. But this time his audience was not grass roots farmers. Elected and appointed highway and governmental officials were the main target. He named this new organization the US Highway 12 Association: Popularly Known as the Yellowstone Trail. His beloved Trail, although truncated to just three states, lived on again. He caused long articles of news and features of US 12 to be published in *South Dakota Hiway Magazine*. The most important topic was the oiling and straightening of US 12.

The autumn of 1938 found the group planning direct lobbying tactics aimed at state highway commissioners. They also phrased double-edged sword letters thanking governors for past work on US 12 and hoping for more. Letters of thanks went to state highway departments for oiling parts of US 12, but they left unsaid their hopes for concrete to avoid backlash.

Although Montana was not officially included in the US 12 organization, the highway department actions from that state were included as news. US 12 formerly terminated at Miles City. In 1939 it was extended through Red Lodge to Yellowstone Park's east entrance. Parmley wrote in the *South Dakota Hiway Magazine*, "This will have a great effect on tourist travel when the rest of South Dakota's stretch of gravel is oiled."[11]   Each bit of news regarding the widening of US 12, the necessity of purchasing more right-of-way, the straightening of the road, and the avoiding of railroad crossings was met with approbation by Parmley and committee. At least *something* was being done for his Trail.

One could see Parmley's hand in the inauguration of essay, song and slogan contests. These were designed for South Dakotans to push for oil to finally cover the gravel, and then (dare one hope?) concrete. Sadly, much of the gravel was to stay until the 1950's before the last section of US 12 in South Dakota saw hard pavement.

One contest slogan submitted in 1938 read, Get us out of the mud by 1940. That one must have hit Parmley hard. Getting out of the mud was the same cry heard throughout the country in 1912 when the Trail Association began. They had come a full circle. Were the efforts of thousands and

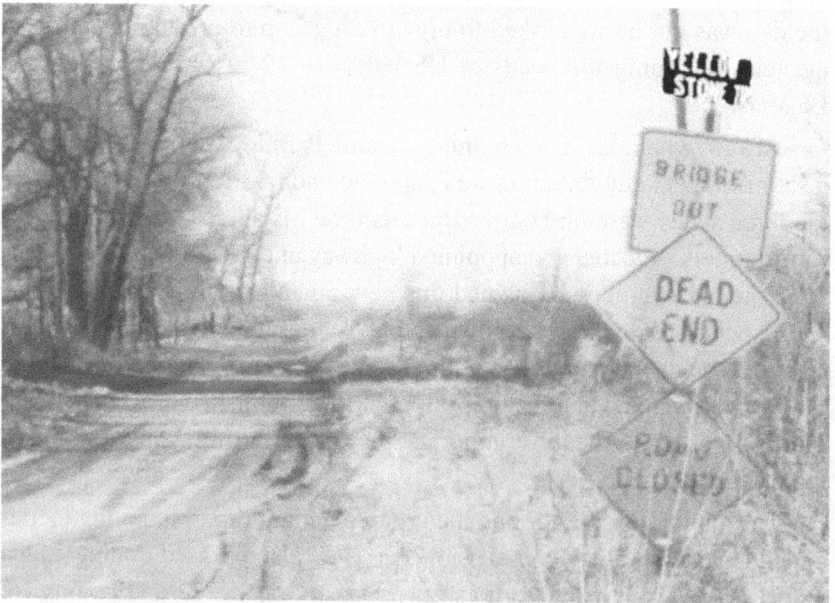

Yellowstone Trail: Bridge Out, Dead End, Road Closed.
Near Hamlet, Indiana Photo by Authors

thousands of people over these almost two decades of the Trail really for naught? By no means!

In the beginning, the route was not always in good condition. It was subject to elements that created a sea of gumbo where a road should have been. But Parmley and his Trail Association played a great national role in creating a mindset that long distance travel could be accomplished by the average auto owner, that the autoist was among friends on the route. Here be dragons no more. Parmley once said that the original promoters of the Yellowstone Trail "builded better than they knew. They did the pioneering which eventually put across a great transcontinental highway."

Joe Parmley "died in his traces" as President of the US Highway 12 Association. He fell in his garden, wrenching his back and shoulder. He never recovered, passing away on December 12, 1940. The J.W. Parmley Museum in Ipswich, South Dakota is located in his house and contains artifacts of his long and illustrious public life.

The J.W. Parmley Museum Ipswich, South Dakota Photo by Authors

Harry Tesch of Waubay, South Dakota remembers, as a little boy, hanging over the fence on his father's farm to watch the noisy Model T's rattle by on the Yellowstone Trail. He would marvel about these strangers with foreign license plates. Where had they come from? Where were they going? What was the world like at the other end of this road? The Yellowstone Trail opened the Northwest to tourists, to markets, and to imagination.

Endnotes

1. Department of Transportation, America's Highways: 1776-1976. A History of the Federal-Aid Program. (Washington, DC:U.S. Govt. Printing Office 1976) 110.

2. Letter from W.J Mulvaney to J.W. Parmley dated March 7, 1928. (South Dakota State Historical Society. Parmley Papers, Folder #2 entitled Yellowstone Trail Association Records 1914-1939.)

3. Aberdeen Evening News December 7, 1929:3.

4. Marmarth Mail September 13, 1929:1.

5. J.W. Parmley, Letter to editors dated July 17, 1930. (South Dakota State Historical Society. Parmley Papers, Folder #2 entitled Yellowstone Trail Association Records 1914-1939.)

6. John B. Davis, "Advantages Offered to Attract Tourists: Improvements Constantly Made", The Aberdeen Sunday American no month or day, 1935.

7. Articles of Incorporation dated Sept. 5, 1930, filed with State of South Dakota. (South Dakota State Historical Society. Parmley Papers, Folder #1, SC10, entitled Yellowstone Highway Association Records 1905-1939.)

8. .Joseph Parmley, "The Yellowstone Highway Association" a white paper. (South Dakota State Historical Society. Parmley Papers Folder #1, SC10, entitled Yellowstone Highway Association. 1905-1939.)

9. Letter from Pfeiffer Paint & Wallpaper of Aberdeen to Joe Parmley. November 19, 1930. (South Dakota State Historical Society. Parmley Papers, Folder #1, SC10, entitled Yellowstone Highway Association. 1905-1939.)

10. Letter from Northern Power & Light Company of Mobridge, South Dakota to Joe Parmley. Dec. 3, 1932. (South Dakota State Historical Society. Parmley Papers, Folder #1, SC10, Yellowstone Highway Association. 1905-1939.)

11. South Dakota Hiway Magazine 1938 (no month cited) 9.

Chapter Six

Driving the Trail Today

Can the Yellowstone Trail be followed nearly 90 years after its founding? To a great extent, yes. In general terms, the cross-country function of the Trail has been replaced by Interstate-90. But it is a mistake to believe that the old Trail has been absorbed by that sleek luge chute which allows us to go across country with no stop signs and to see absolutely nothing but distant scenery.

Today almost all of the old route is on the slower, less traveled and more interesting roads. Driving the Trail today allows the tourist to explore the history surrounding the Trail, to find old inns, hotels, garages, and ghost towns. Some sections of the Trail in the West have remained little changed and are a delight to visit. Some parts of the original Trail have reverted to farm land and some are overlain by new highways or buildings, but most of the Trail has just been updated to varying standards. Many little sections are still named "Yellowstone Trail." In the East the Trail can be located along the old Boston Post Road, and on many miles of US 20. Near Hamlet, Indiana the Trail runs parallel with one version of the Lincoln Highway, both on quiet backroads.

The following pages provide maps of the Trail as it passed through 13 states on its 1921 route. Several of the more interesting, driveable portions are noted. We invite you to find a bit of the Trail and use your imagination to experience the slower life of the early 1900's.

This brief introductory book cannot specify all of the hundreds of highway numbers, turns, and changes over time that comprise the Yellowstone Trail across our nation. These maps tell you where the road went as a history, not a complete road guide. A much larger book is being prepared by the authors which will contain a mile-by-mile location of the presently driveable portions of the old Yellowstone Trail.

Washington

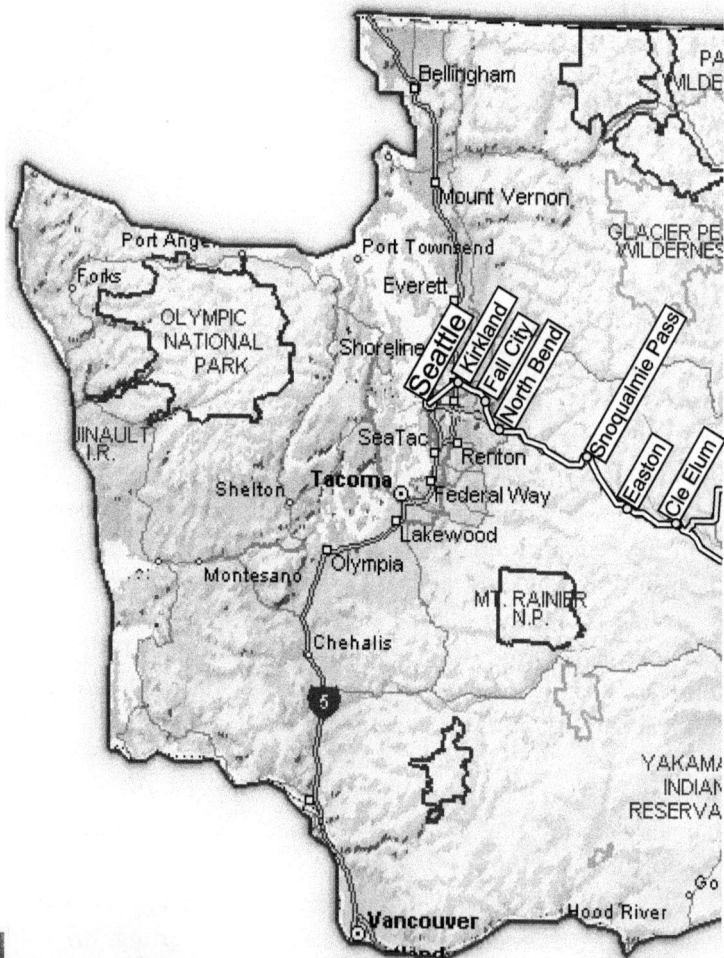

An original piece of the Trail is being used every day. It is called the **Red Brick Road** with many of the original red bricks still in place. The road, a King County Landmark, is 196th Ave. NE, between state #202 and Union Hill Road near Redmond and Kirkland, Washington. It is about one mile long.

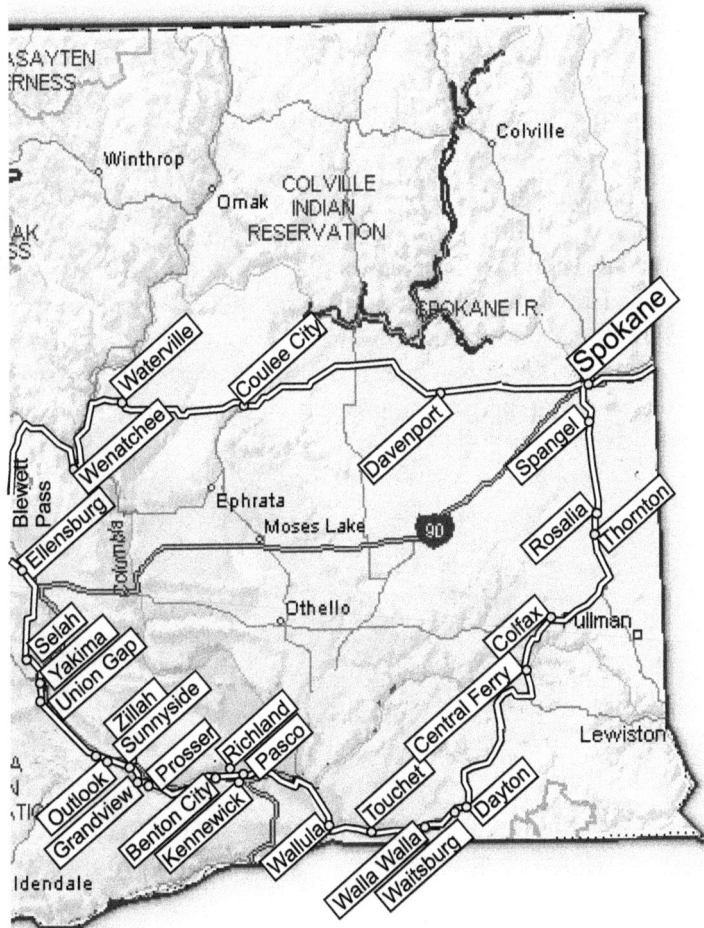

From about 1915 to 1925, the Yellowstone Trail in Washington followed the "southern" route through Walla Walla. Going north from Yakima to Ellensburg it followed WA 823 to just north of Selah, then North Wenas Road along Wenas Creek. **North Wenas Road** becomes **Untanum Road** and drops into Ellensburg from the south. This 43 mile driveable section of the Yellowstone Trail appears to follow the original route, but it is now gravel rather than the original dirt surface. It is an excellent drive during which one can visualize travel in 1920.

In 1925 the Trail was changed from the "southern route" through Walla Walla to a "northern route" from Spokane through Wenatchee to Cle Elum.   This was one of two major changes in the route of the Trail during its lifetime. The reason for the change is undocumented, but was evidently made to shorten

Wenas Road

the route considerably as soon as the road conditions of the north route were acceptable. This had always been the route of the National Parks Highway. Just south of Blewett the modern highway, US 97, loops to the east around **Blewett Pass**. The 11 mile section over the Pass is a driveable portion of the Trail, although it is very narrow, mountainous, beautiful, and challenging to the urban driver.

Coeur d'Alene, Idaho is one of America's most beautiful cities and the Yellowstone Trail followed what is perhaps the best scenic route through and east of the city. Much of the route has retained the name **"E. Yellowstone Trail"** making it fairly easy to follow, but the modern pavement detracts from the historical experience. The original route followed Couer d'Alene

*"Yellowstone Trail" east
of Coeur d'Alene*

Lake Road south from Sherman Ave. at a point a block or two west of I-90 Exit 15. E. Yellowstone Trail is met in about four miles. It can be followed for about 6 miles until it meets I-90 again at Exit 22.

I-90 crosses the Idaho-Montana border and the Bitterroot Mountains along **Lookout Pass**. I-90 totally obliterates an interesting section of the Yellowstone Trail route used after about 1922. After years of negotiating between Shoshone County, Idaho and Mineral County, Montana, a passable road over Lookout Pass was completed. The counties blamed each other for delays. The exact date of completion is obscure, reports varying from 1922 to 1925. People apparently just started driving on it while the work, somewhat unevenly, proceeded.

Fortunately, the beautiful, driveable, original 1915-1922 route remains. It is the **Mullan Pass/Randolph Creek** route. (Note: Mullan Pass, in spite of its name, is not on the Mullan Military Road, the first wagon road to be built across the Bitterroots.) The route is gravel, rather than dirt as it was then, but it recalls for today's driver the roads around 1920. It travels through a delightful forest across the spine of the Bitterroots.

To find the old route from the west, use I-90 Exit 69 near Mullan and find Old US 10. Follow Old US 10 to the east. It turns into Larson Road. Near Shoshone Park follow a branch to the south that is Old Yellowstone Trail. East of Mullan Pass, in Montana, the road becomes Randolph Creek Road (marked as FR 286 in places), ending at I-90 Exit 5, just west of Bryson and east of the ghost town of Taft. This 13-mile distance is easily driveable, but a detailed map (or GPS) is desirable in order to avoid turning onto logging or mining roads. Traffic is nearly non-existent, so let someone know when you will be back.

An anonymous gentleman recalled his trip on this road in 1923 or 1924: "The road was a very narrow dirt road which wound up the mountainsides. It offered breath-taking scenery, but required considerable skill from the driver of those early cars. As we approached the pass's summit we were greeted with the view of a "house car" which had overturned and rolled some distance down a steep slope."

Idaho

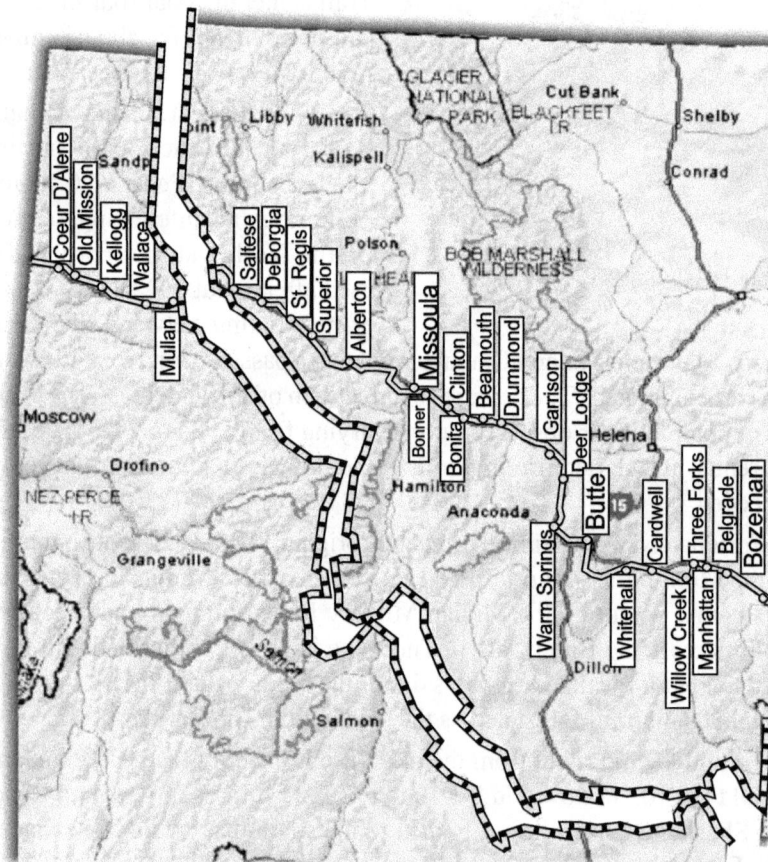

Between St. Regis and DeBorgia, Montana is a paved, hilly, beautiful 11-mile section of the old Yellowstone Trail over the **Camel's Hump**. The only reminders of life on the Trail around 1922 are the remnants of Cabin City, which was a popular, rough-hewn camp for hunters.

Near **Three Forks**, Montana, close to the Lewis and Clark Trail, there

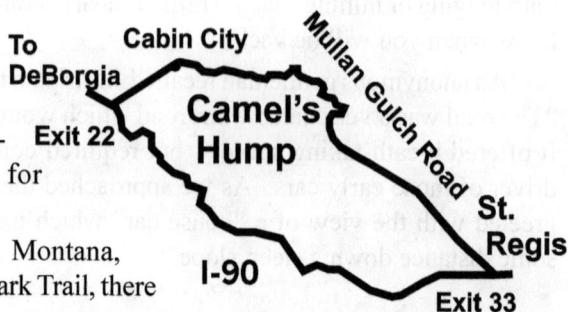

Montana

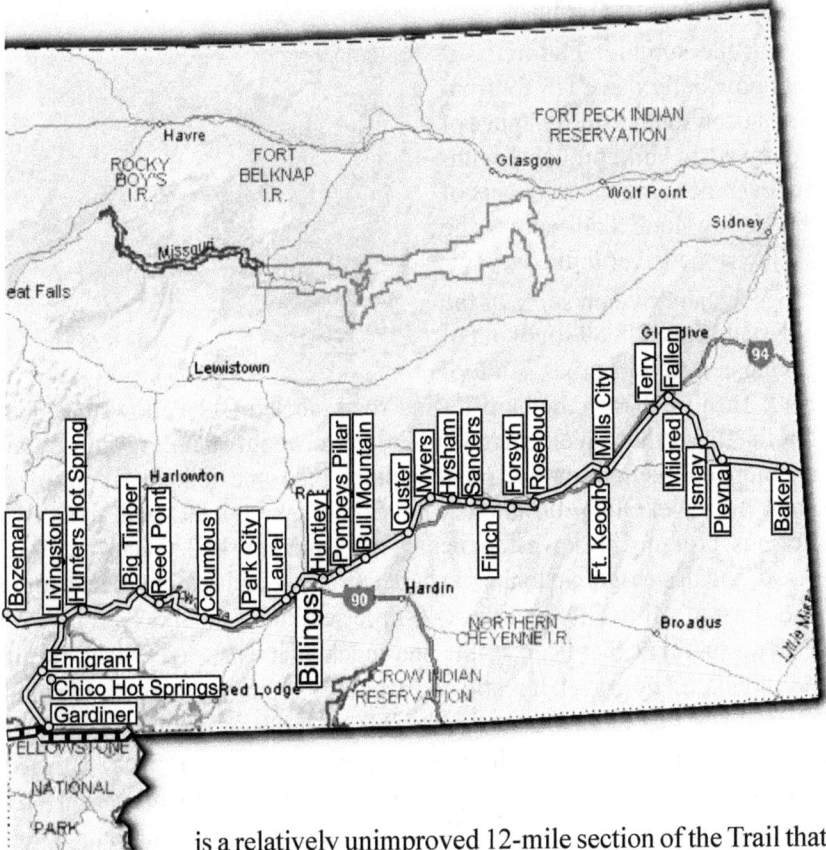

is a relatively unimproved 12-mile section of the Trail that still bears the name Yellowstone Trail Road and, in places, Old Yellowstone Trail. Follow Willow Creek Road from Three Forks to Willow Creek, Woodside Road south and west of town for a very short distance, then join Old Yellowstone Trail. This is a dirt road, easy to drive unless, as in 1915, it is wet; then even a Jeep tends to slip to one side or the other. US 287 is met just north of Harrison. US 287 and then MT 2, can be taken north to return to I-90.

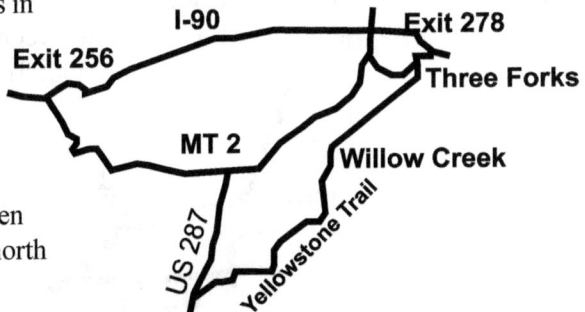

From **Livingston**, Montana, passenger trains would take **Yellowstone Park** visitors to the North Entrance at Gardiner.

In the summer hundreds of cars now daily drive US 89 from Livingston south to the entrance of Yellowstone Park, probably without even noticing the remnants of the Yellowstone Trail across the Yellowstone River to the west.

You can drive on some of the old road. Take US 89 south out of Livingston to four miles south of

Camel's Hump

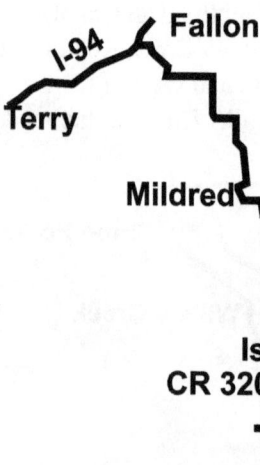

I-90. Turn west onto the hard-to-find-road labeled Old Yellowstone Trail North. Enjoy the gravel, old road to Emigrant, about 16 miles south. There are more old sections of the Trail to explore, but some of them are now dead ends. To travel Old Yellowstone Trail South, take US 89 south to Corwin Springs, crossing back west to pick up the Trail, now called Gardiner Back Road, and drive right up to the old park entrance - and seldom meet another car. East of Miles City there is a 40-mile section of the old Trail between **Plevna to Terry** that is driveable and much as it was, except that dirt has been replaced by gravel. It is still an adventure. A sign at Miles City reminds the traveler that there are no services for 76 miles to Baker, nor are there any between Plevna and Fallon. So be prepared. From Plevna to Ismay, through semiarid ranch territory, the route is not well marked but there are few decision points. Stop at Westmore, a ghost town, and roam among the ruins, imagining a town of 80 years ago big enough to have a railroad side track. At Ismay, there are few people, 23 by one count, but they are proud of their town and have erected signs marking the locations of former buildings. J.E. Prindle, second president of the Yellowstone Trail Association and real estate agent, made his home here and it, too, is marked. The road from Ismay to Mildred, the Ismay-

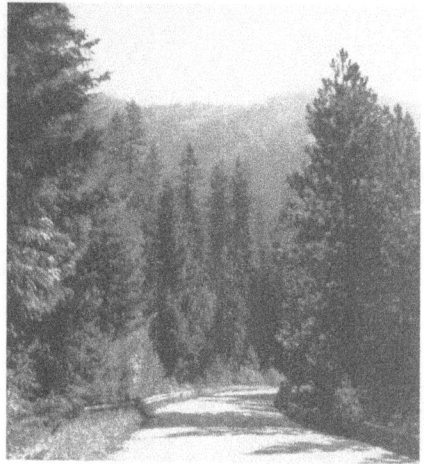

Mildred Cut Across, closely follows the route of the Yellowstone Trail, however the new road runs at some angles and "cuts across" corners. Today, Mildred hosts a few homes and a grain elevator, but not much else. From Mildred to Terry follow Mildred Road, then Highway 340 into Fallon, where I-94 can be found.

In North and South Dakota, the original roads used by the Trail followed section lines wherever possible yielding a jagged route near the Milwaukee Road tracks. The modern road, US 12 in North and South Dakota, uses smooth curves leaving the cut-off bits of the Trail to remain relatively unchanged. One such example of a cut-off bit is near **Haynes, North Dakota,** which is also interesting because of the

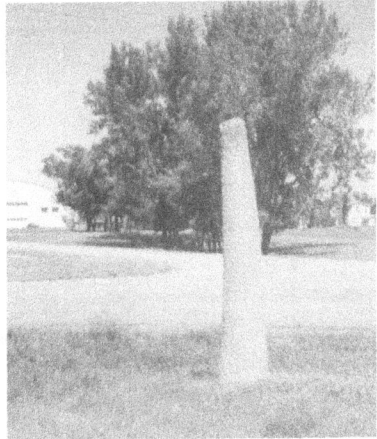

Haynes, North Dakota

presumably original yellow stone Trail marker in the middle of town. From the east on US 12, one mile north of the South Dakota border and .5 miles north of the rail crossing turn west on poor road which becomes Railway St. and enter Haynes. From the west, turn south to Haynes at the intersection at which ND 8 enters from the north. The total cut-off is about 6 miles.

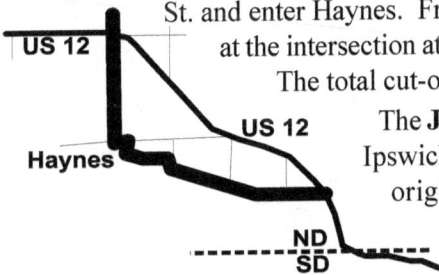

The **J.W. Parmley Historical Museum,** Ipswich, South Dakota is located in the original Parmley home and contains a general historical collection as well as artifacts specifically related to the Yellowstone Trail. (See picture on page 73.) In a small park near US 12 is an arch commemorating the Trail. Between **Aberdeen and Ipswich, South Dakota,** 13 of the 26 original miles of the **Parmley Highway,** while now paved, have not been overlaid by the US 12 route. This is the road which, in 1912, began the whole Yellowstone Trail movement. The road runs west out of Aberdeen on 133 St. (or County 12W), turns south on 369 Ave., around Mina Lake and the Mina State Recreation Area, just north of Mina where it rejoins US 12. Mina Lake is still officially called Lake Parmley on US Geological Service maps. In 1932 Joe Parmley was the instigator of the dam and resultant lake. The project was completed in 1950.

North Dakota

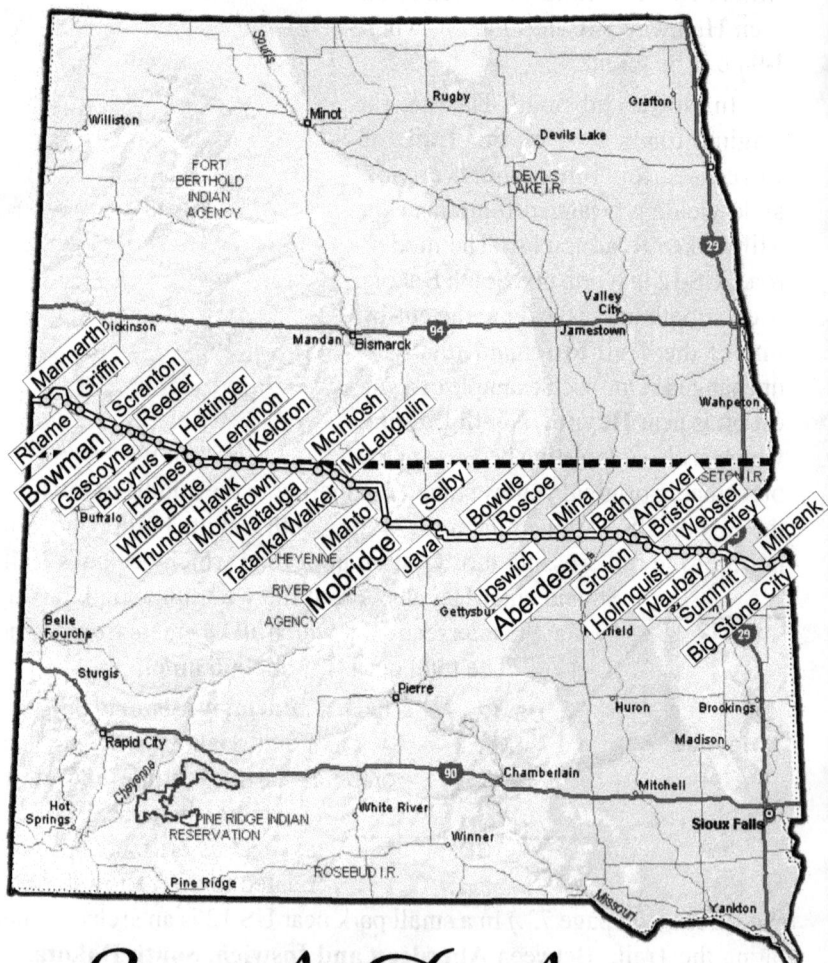

South Dakota

There is a revived interest in promoting the Yellowstone Trail in South Dakota as a tourist attraction. The Aberdeen Convention and Visitors Bureau has produced a travel brochure that features Yellowstone Trail cities. They are also working to mark the Trail with the familiar black arrow on yellow.

The creator of the **Vinegar Museum** in Roslyn, South Dakota, 12 miles north of Webster and the Trail, tried to motivate a coast to coast interest in

Minnesota

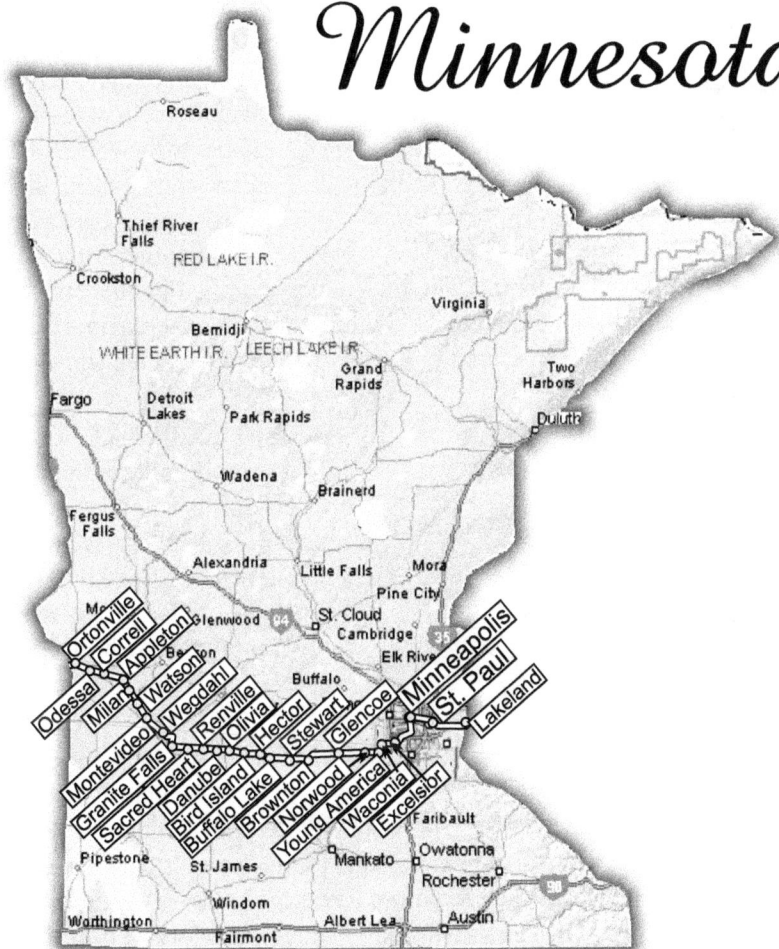

the Trail as an attraction for the historical tourist. The third purpose of the Association lives on - to attract tourists!

In **Minnesota**, between Montevideo and Norwood, US 212 follows the general route of the Trail. Here, as in the Dakotas, the new highway curves through the section line jags of the old, leaving small distances of the old much as they were. Through Minnesota state legislation some years ago, US 212 was designated "The Yellowstone Trail" and appropriate marking was specified. Those signs, however, are few. From Norwood, the Trail to Minneapolis followed, generally, the route now marked MN 5, MN 7, CR 25, Lake St., and Hennepin Ave.

The Falls of St. Anthony

When the Association was formed and announced that the route would run from the Twin Cities to the Yellowstone Park, they picked as the starting point the Falls of St. Anthony in the Mississippi River in Minneapolis. The falls, much modified by man, may be viewed today from about four blocks southeast of the Hennepin Ave. bridge across the Mississippi. The Trail followed Hennepin Ave., then University Ave. into St. Paul.

The Old St. Croix River bridge, with remaining causeway on the far side.

East from the Twin Cities, I-94 generally follows the route of the Trail to Eau Claire, Wisconsin. The Trail crossed the St. Croix River at the Minnesota/ Wisconsin border just north of the present Interstate bridge. The causeway built almost across the whole of the river from Hudson, Wisconsin is still in place. It can be visited by driving a few blocks north in Hudson along the river.

In Wisconsin, several convention and tourist bureaus between Chippewa Falls and Stevens Point have joined forces to use the Yellowstone Trail as a focus for their tourist advertising: another revival of one of the original purposes of the Yellowstone Trail Association! The group received a state grant to advertise their 140-mile section of the Trail. The local historians started the new interest in the Trail and motivated an annual parade in Thorp featuring cars which might have driven the Trail. Following their lead, the new convention and tourist bureau initiative will sponsor an antique car "Trail Run" along the Trail.

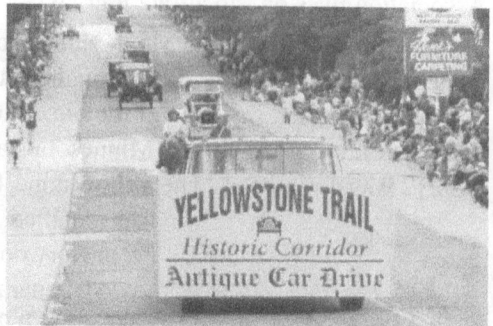

YELLOWSTONE TRAIL
Historic Corridor
Antique Car Drive

Thorp, Wisconsin

Wisconsin

The Trail is not visible much in its original form in Wisconsin, but a few places offer glimpses into the past. The Yellowstone Garage on 1st Avenue in Stanley was there in 1915 and still does business today. A Bar in Owen features a large "R" on its brick wall, indicating that the Trail turned right at that corner in 1915. A gravel road through just south of Hewitt, just east of Marshfield, is called Yellowstone Avenue and follows the earliest route of the Trail. The more urban southeastern part of the state has few remaining signs of the Trail.

Illinois Indiana

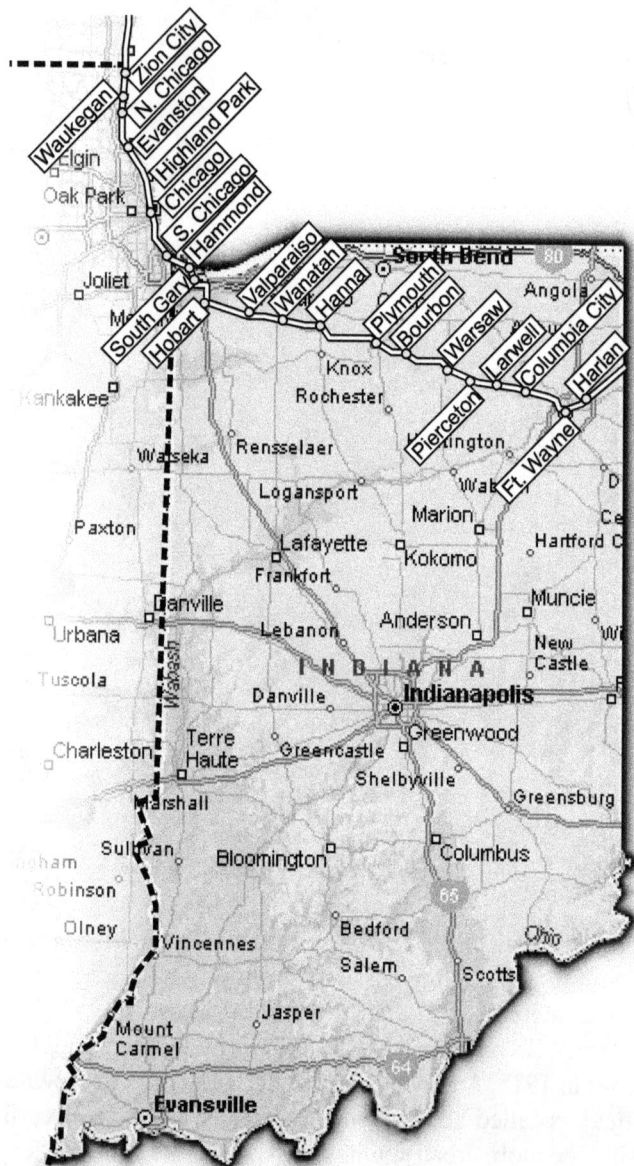

Zion City
N. Chicago
Evanston
Highland Park
Chicago
S. Chicago
Hammond
Waukegan
Elgin
Oak Park

Joliet

South Gary
Hobart
Valparaiso
Wanatah
Hanna
Plymouth
Bourbon
Warsaw
Larwell
Columbia City
Harlan

South Bend
Angola

Knox
Rochester
Pierceton
Lexington
Ft. Wayne

Kankakee
Watseka
Rensselaer
Logansport
Wab
D
Marion
Ce

Paxton
Lafayette
Kokomo
Hartford C

Frankfort
Danville
Muncie

Urbana
Lebanon
Anderson
New
Castle
Wi

Tuscola
I N D I A N A
Danville
Indianapolis

Wabash

Charleston
Terre
Haute
Greencastle
Greenwood
Greensburg

Shelbyville

Marshall

Sullivan
Bloomington
Columbus

gham
Robinson

Olney
Bedford
Ohio

Vincennes
Salem
Scotts

Jasper

Mount
Carmel

64

Evansville

80

66

Pennsylvania
Ohio

East of Wisconsin, the Yellowstone Trail Association marked the Trail with its familiar yellow circle with the black arrow, provided road information to enquiring tourists, and worked to increase tourist traffic, but it was never as active as it was in the West. As late as 1919, the annual Folder states that it "... makes no claim to having any intensive organization, or special information in any of that section of the road ... east of Sandusky, Ohio.

Yet the Trail had a substantial presence and was widely known. There were Yellowstone Trail Association travel bureaus in Fort Wayne, Indiana, Cleveland, Ohio and Schenectady, New York. The Automobile Blue Books,

New York

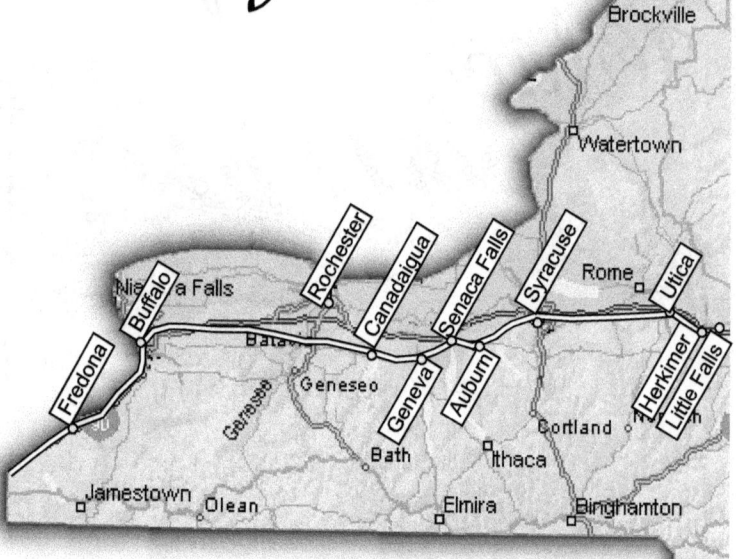

among other guides, identified those roads which were part of the Yellowstone Trail. Restaurants and garages included references to the Trail. For instance, Hicksville, Ohio had a Yellowstone Restaurant which maintained the name for several decades. Many streets and roads have retained the Yellowstone name. Near Hamlet, Indiana a Yellowstone Trail Road meets old US 30, also the Trail at one time. In Valparaiso, there is a historic intersection of Yellowstone Trail and Lincoln Highway. In Massachusetts, US 20 has replaced the Trail. A 3.7-mile "detour" from US 20 follows a stretch of the old Yellowstone Trail east of Huntington. It allows the imagination to recreate the 1920's. From Huntington, follow Basket Street to Fisk Avenue/Old Chester Road to Old State Road. Here, US 20 is rejoined.

The Yellowstone Trail through Batavia, New York. Post card view.

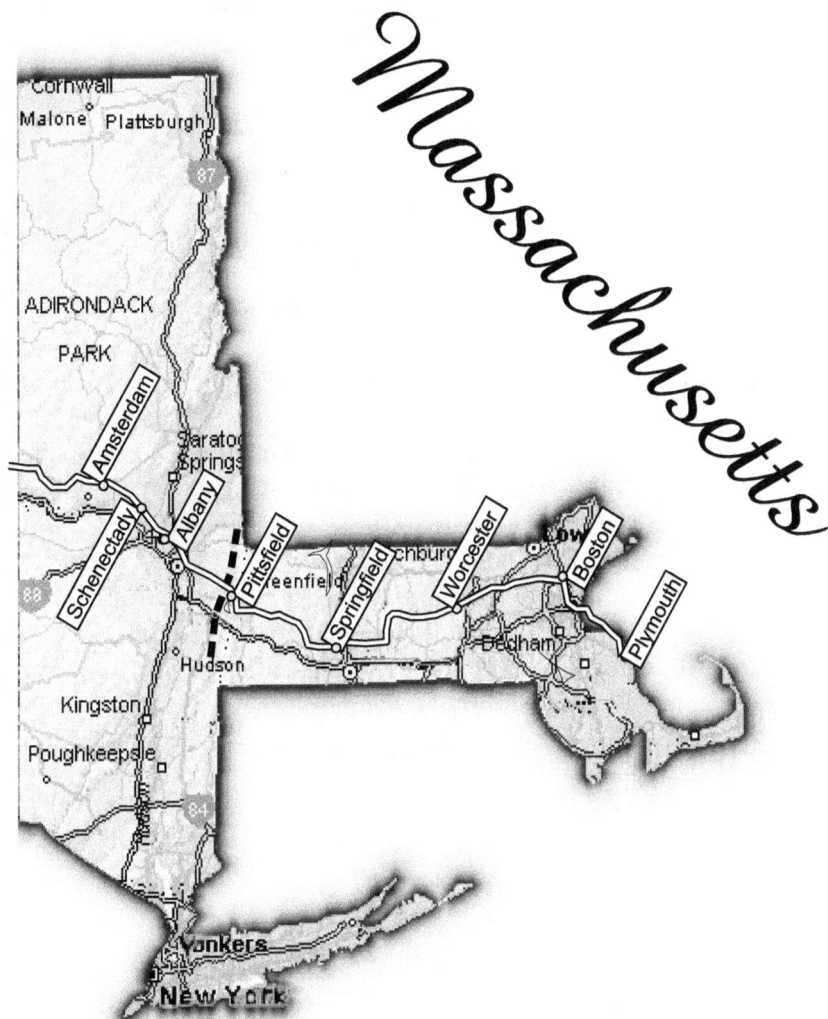

It is difficult today to find many pieces of the old Trail east of Wisconsin that are as they were in the 1920's. By following the route meticulously, the authors have ended up in major oil company distribution sites, in a maze of roads outside of Boston, lost, and in the very heart of large cities' hotel districts. Little in these urban places is reminiscent of the old Trail. But yet, most of the route is still on the quieter back roads that make travel a joy - and slow.

Joe Parmley would be content.

Introducing

The Yellowstone Trail

There is no mother lode of information about the Yellowstone Trail. One hundred years has dimmed memories and hid documents. So, armed with a tape recorder, a global positioning system, scanner and computer, the authors prowled through small town libraries, museums, attics, microfilmed newspapers, and universities' archives. They interviewed scores of people who once knew the Trail or who possessed some of the old road bed in their back fields, the depressions still dimly visible in their pastures. We are grateful for the help of many dozens of people who enthusiastically searched their memories, attics and archives.

A glimpse of the product of many years of research is in this introductory book. A much larger, comprehensive and, we hope, authoritative history of the Trail and its sponsoring Association is anticipated to be published soon. It will contain detailed maps for every mile between Plymouth Rock and Seattle, dozens of contemporary pictures, and newspaper articles about the Trail. It will be a complete guide to driving the Trail to discover its history. Contact the publishers to request notification of publication.

Alice A. Ridge

John Wm. Ridge

Single copies of this book are $9.95 plus $3.00 shipping. Contact the publisher for shipping costs of multiple copies or the price of copies for resale.

Other related publications are availale, including:

1919 Route Folder of the Yellowstone Trail Association (annotated and reprinted). 4.25 x 11 inches. 32 pages. $4.00 plus $1.00 shipping.

Yellowstone Trail Publishers
PO Box 65
Altoona, WI 54720-0065

Or, visit the Web site:
www.yellowstonetrail.org
for current information

www.ingramcontent.com/pod-product-compliance
Lightning Source LLC
Chambersburg PA
CBHW071015040426
42443CB00007B/791